D1510776

WORKER DISLOCATION
Case Studies of Causes and Cures

Robert F. Cook
Editor

1987

W. E. Upjohn Institute for Employment Research

Library of Congress Cataloging-in-Publication Data

Worker dislocation.

1. Layoff systems—United States—Case studies.
2. Plant shutdowns—United States—Case studies
3. Employees, Dismissal of—United States—Case
studies. I. Cook, Robert F., 1943-   . II. W.E.
Upjohn Institute for Employment Research.
HD5708.55.U6W67   1987   331.13'7973   87-31717
ISBN 0-88099-053-8
ISBN 0-88099-052-X (pbk.)

PREFACE

In October 1983, Westat, Inc. undertook a process study of the implementation of Titles IIA and III of the Job Training Partnership Act of 1982 (JTPA) for the U.S. Department of Labor. The study observed the implementation of the program in a randomly selected sample of 20 states and 40 Service Delivery Areas (SDAs) within those states. These observations were carried out by a network of field associates, university professors and researchers, located in the areas of study. The study covered the initial transition year of the program (October 1, 1983 through June 30, 1984) as well as the first full program year of operation (July 1, 1984 through June 30, 1985).

In January 1984, Westat carried out the collection of information on the universe of Title III Dislocated Worker Projects operating in the 50 states. The analysis of this information indicated that a majority of the Title III funding was going to program operators outside the SDA system that provided training for economically disadvantaged individuals under Title IIA of the JTPA program. Therefore, Westat undertook a series of case studies to provide information on the implementation of specific Title III Dislocated Worker Projects at the local project level.

This volume contains case studies of nine Dislocated Worker projects selected to vary according to the program operator, the eligible population, the services provided, and the labor market in which the projects operated. All the projects were thought to be "successful" by the states and program operators. The emphasis in the selection was on relative effectiveness—what works for whom under what circumstances—and the objective was to provide information to those interested in what the states were doing in their Title III programs and in the activities that might be applicable to particular dislocated worker populations.

Specific selection of the individual projects was based on the inventory of all Title III projects carried out as a part of the overall study. The case studies were prepared by field associates located in the areas in which the projects were operating, following an initial assessment of the projects by the associates.

To provide consistency and assist in the editing process, Westat staff accompanied the case study authors on their field visits. In fact, to aid in the refinement of the report form, one of the case studies (the Hillsborough Cone-Mills case study) was carried out by Wayne Turnage, who, at that time, was part of the Westat staff. In addition, special thanks for effort above and beyond that called for by the honoraria are due to Professor Lawrence Wohl of Gustavus Adolphus College, who undertook the observation of the first project (the Minnesota Iron Range Project) and wrote the case study that provided the model for the other authors.

Beyond the efforts of the individual case study authors, it is necessary to acknowledge the willingness of the individual staff members of the projects to participate, to supply information and to discuss with the case study authors not only the successes but also the "warts" in their projects.

Indeed, we encountered no problems with cooperation in any of the project sites. Draft copies of the individual case studies were sent to the appropriate officials in each of the project locations and comments were, to the extent possible, accommodated. Perhaps the nicest comment received (from the Cummins project in Indiana) was, "You people listened."

Finally, initial editing of the case studies was performed by David L. Aiken, who died in December 1986. This volume is dedicated to his memory.

Robert F. Cook
November 1987

This book was prepared with assistance from the Office of Research and Evaluation of the Employment and Training Administration, U.S. Department of Labor, under contract No. 99-3-0584-75-104-01. No points of view or opinions expressed should be ascribed to the Department of Labor or Westat, Inc.

CONTENTS

1
Introduction

The Dislocated Worker Problem

Since roughly 1980, the United States has experienced job losses in a number of basic and secondary industries resulting from technological change, world competition, and worldwide supply/demand imbalances adversely affecting prices of basic raw materials and foodstuffs. These factors have led not only to large scale layoffs in basic industries (oil and gas production, primary metals), and manufacturing and textiles, but to bankruptcies and decline in agriculture and related industries. The result has been that large numbers of experienced (often unionized and well paid) workers have lost not only their jobs but the prospects of reemployment in the industries where they have worked for most of their lives. They are the dislocated workers.

The numbers of workers affected were initially and continue to be in some dispute. Early proxy estimates suggested that, given reemployment following the recession, the range of the number of dislocated workers was 300,000 to 815,000.[1] Subsequently, a special supplement to the January 1984 *Current Population Survey* (CPS) questionnaire, analyzed by the Bureau of Labor Statistics (BLS), resulted in an estimate that 5.1 million people who had been employed at least three years in a particular firm had lost jobs between January 1979 and January 1984 as the result of a plant closing, major layoff, or the permanent loss of their particular job (the definition of a dislocated worker). Of these workers, 3.5 million had collected unemployment benefits, 1.3 million were looking for work in January 1984 and another 700,000 had left the labor force.[2] More recently, using the Bureau of Labor

Statistics data, the General Accounting Office (GAO) has estimated that 2.3 million workers were dislocated annually between 1979 and 1984.[3] A subsequent, comprehensive report by the Office of Technology Assessment accepted the CPS/BLS estimates.[4]

In response to the problem of dislocated workers, the Congress in October 1982 included in the Job Training Partnership Act, Title III, which was designed to respond to the problems of experienced but laid off workers.[5]

The Purpose of This Volume

This volume was designed with two basic objectives. The first is purely descriptive: what is being done in a set of varied Dislocated Worker Projects funded under Title III of the Job Training Partnership Act (JTPA). Title III concentrates on experienced workers who have lost jobs due to a layoff or plant closing, rather than inexperienced, economically disadvantaged individuals. Therefore, a straightforward description of what is being done may be of use to policymakers and others interested in employment and training policy and the problem of worker dislocation.

The second objective is to provide technical assistance to program operators or potential program operators by describing the experience of others who have operated these programs. The case studies examine some of the things that have been tried, and what has been learned from these experiences.

This chapter describes the nature of the Title III program under JTPA, provides background on how the particular projects were selected as case studies for this volume, and indicates the general nature of these projects. Each of the following nine chapters presents an individual case study written in a consistent format. The final chapter then looks across the case studies and examines what has been learned. Specific attention is given to the question of relative effectiveness: ''What works for whom under what set of circumstances?'' It is hoped that this examination will provide an understanding of the problem of worker dislocation, as well as the results of experimentation with various solutions to that dilemma.

Title III of JTPA

The Dislocated Worker Program, authorized by Title III of the Job Training Partnership Act, has an entirely different focus from the rest of the Act. While other titles of the Act provide training resources for the economically disadvantaged, Title III is designed to assist experienced workers who have lost their jobs or are at risk of losing their jobs because of plant closings and layoffs due to technological change and world competition.

A major element of Title III is the role it gives the states in designing and implementing the program. Many responsibilities that were traditionally functions of the federal government have been shifted to the state level. The states have almost complete authority over how the program is targeted, how resources are distributed, and what services will be provided.

The legislation requires that 70 percent of all Title III funds be devoted to training activities. In addition, the U.S. Department of Labor (DOL) built into the Title III budget an estimated cost per slot of $6,610 ($3,305 per participant) for transition year (October 1983 to June 30, 1984) 1984 and $6,864 for program year (July 1, 1984 to June 30, 1985) 1984 ($3,432 per participant). These figures carried an implicit assumption that dislocated workers require significant retraining in order to become reemployed.

Many Title III eligibles held high paying jobs within a firm for a number of years. However, the skills learned in those occupations may be firm-specific and not transferrable to other jobs that pay similarly high wages. Therefore, project operators may find it necessary to provide counseling aimed at reducing participants' wage expectations. Other dislocated workers are in need of financial assistance and personal counseling. Still other eligibles prefer strategies that produce immediate employment, such as job search and on-the-job training (OJT) as opposed to long-term training programs that might result in new career opportunities. Finally, in attempting to maintain seniority, skill levels and income, others may return to the same industry from which they were laid off or wait "for the plant gates to reopen."

Allocation Provisions

Federal funds for Title III programs are allocated in two ways. The principal method, by which 75 percent of the money is distributed to the states, is a formula allocation based on three factors:

(1)   the state's relative share of the number of all unemployed persons in the country;

(2)   the state's share of the number of "excess" unemployed persons in the country, with "excess" defined as those above 4.5 percent of the civilian labor force; and

(3)   the state's relative share of persons unemployed for longer than 15 weeks.

Each state must match these federal funds with an equal amount of nonfederal public or private funds, but the amount of the required match is reduced by 10 percent for each percentage point that the state's average unemployment rate exceeded the national unemployment rate in the prior fiscal year.

Second, the Secretary of Labor can allocate up to 25 percent of the Title III funds at his discretion. States apply for these funds to meet special needs beyond those that can be met from the formula allocation. No state matching is required for grants from this discretionary fund.

Sources of Title III Funds

Title III programs in the early stages of JTPA were funded from four different sources:

(1)   For federal fiscal year 1983, more than $18 million was distributed to the states by formula. Later, a second allocation

of over $63 million was made from the Emergency Jobs Bill (Public Law 98-8).

(2) In September 1983, the Secretary of Labor announced that the $27.5 million discretionary fund was available to assist states particularly hard hit by conditions that led to worker dislocation.

(3) During October and November 1983, more than $70 million was distributed by formula for the 9-month transition period, from October 1983, through June 30, 1984. Another $24 million was reserved for discretionary funding by the Secretary.

(4) Funding for the 12-month program year 1984 (July 1, 1984 through June 30, 1985) of $223 million (of which 25 percent was held in the Secretary's reserve) brought the total amount of Title III funding available to well over $400 million.

Program Targeting

Governors are allowed considerable latitude in defining dislocated workers eligible for the Title III program in their states. The clear intention of Congress, however, was to concentrate Title III on experienced workers who have recently been laid off from jobs to which they are unlikely to return, rather than on persons who have just entered or re-entered the labor force. Section 302(a) of the law authorizes the states to designate eligible groups from among those who:

(1) have been terminated or laid off or who have received a notice of termination or layoff from employment, are eligible for or have exhausted their entitlement to unemployment compensation, and are unlikely to return to their previous industry or occupation;

(2) have been terminated, or who have received a notice of termination of employment, as a result of any permanent closure of a plant or facility; or

(3) are long-term unemployed and have limited opportunities for employment or reemployment in the same or a similar occupa-

tion in the area in which they reside, including any older individuals who may have substantial barriers to employment by reason of age.

These provisions, in effect, restrict Title III eligibility to the unemployed who have job experience. They thereby exclude new labor force entrants and welfare recipients with little employment history, two groups that form a prominent part of the eligible population for Title IIA.

Persons exhausting their unemployment insurance (UI) benefits are specifically mentioned as a target group. Stress on these unemployed persons is reinforced by Section 306, which specifies that UI benefits to an individual may be a source of nonfederal match. JTPA also suggests that states might target "substantial" groups of eligible individuals. Such targeting may be geographic, occupational, industrial, or along other lines, and may result in projects designed to serve these groups, rather than providing coverage to all individuals eligible on a statewide basis.

These provisions parallel the targeting of the Area Redevelopment Act of the early 1960s and the early period of the Manpower Demonstration Training Act from 1962 to 1967. The major differences rest in a governor's latitude to shape the service programs and to distribute the funds among programs, services, and areas of the state.

The following three provisions explicitly limit this discretion:

(1)   Section 305 requires that Title III programs, other than statewide or industrywide programs, must be submitted for review and recommendations by the Private Industry Councils (PICs) and elected officials of any Service Delivery Area (SDA) in which they operate. If local authorities do not support the program, but the state chooses to operate it nonetheless, the state must document the reasons for the decision.

(2)   Section 306 requires "full consultation" with a labor organization before any Title III program provides services to a substantial portion of its members.

(3)   Section 308 explicitly reiterates that the statewide coordination plan mandated under Section 121 must address Title III activities.

The wide discretion allowed state officials may be illustrated by the issue of Title III allocation policy within the state. At one extreme, the state can choose to allocate all Title III federal formula funds to SDAs or units of governments by some state formula, reserving to the state the responsibility of ensuring that the money is spent on allowable activities for eligible individuals. At the other extreme, the state may use its Title III allocation to fund a single-site project serving a narrowly defined target group of eligible persons. Between these two extremes exist a multitude of options for targeting by geographic area, industry, or occupation.

Selection of Case Study Projects

The immediate purpose of this study was to produce a series of short case studies of individual Title III dislocated worker projects. Nine Title III projects were selected to represent a variety of circumstances: projects that are firm- and industry-specific as well as those that serve all Title III eligible individuals within a given labor market area; those that provide a variety of services from job search to classroom training, and from OJT to counseling; those operating in different labor markets, from a declining industry in an otherwise thriving labor market to ones operating within a generally depressed labor market; and projects operated by different organizations and with different strategies for providing services to dislocated workers.

We therefore selected relatively large projects (500 to 1,000 planned participants during the transition year) that appeared to be operating successfully and represented a range of different service strategies, target groups and labor market conditions.

The U.S. Department of Labor budgeted per participant costs for transition year 1984 and program year 1984 assuming that dislocated workers needed substantial retraining. Others have argued that the primary service under Title III should be job search assistance or that the primary need among experienced workers is for job finding skills and counseling aimed at reducing wage expectations. Although allowed, and used in some cases, relocation may be appropriate in generally depressed labor markets, but most studies have indicated that individual participants are not interested in relocation. Early reports indicated that potential participants were interested in jobs (implying a reliance on job search and OJT rather than classroom training). Yet, some projects are emphasizing relatively long classroom training programs through community colleges and vocational schools.

Different projects may have different eligible populations that require different services. For example, a plant shutdown may idle more experienced and older workers, while a partial layoff may idle younger, less experienced workers who may be more like Title IIA eligible (economically disadvantaged) participants. This may affect the particular mix of services selected by the individual projects.

The Design of the Project

In January 1984, Westat, as a part of a process study of the implementation of the Job Training Partnership Act, undertook the collection of information on the universe of Title III projects in the 50 states.[6] That universe, along with additional information collected from the states by the field associates for the process study, formed the basis for the selection of the Dislocated Worker Projects for these case studies.

No attempt has been made to argue that these projects are representative of the universe of Title III Dislocated Worker Projects in the 50 states. Rather, the projects were selected to vary along four dimensions: the grant recipient or program operator; the eligible population for the project; the kinds of services provided by the project; and the nature of the labor market in which the program operated. Exhibit 1-1 lists the projects covered in this volume as well as certain information on each of them along the dimensions outlined above.

As an introduction to the projects, it is useful to look at the range of grant recipients—the organizations that received the funds to operate the specific project from the state formula funds or the Secretary's discretionary money.

The Cummins Engine Company, a private firm in Columbus, Indiana, is the grant recipient for a project that operates in three counties in southern Indiana. The actual program operation, however, is subcontracted to another private firm.

The Metropolitan Pontiac Retraining and Employment program in Pontiac, Michigan is a joint union-management program with two co-directors, one from the management of General Motors Corporation and one from the United Auto Workers.

The Minnesota Iron Range project is operated by the Northeast Minnesota Office of Job Training, the grant recipient and administrative entity for a seven-county Service Delivery Area in the northeast quadrant of that state.

The Job Search Assistance, Inc. project in Missouri is operated by a private not-for-profit firm under subcontract to the Division of Manpower Planning which administers JTPA in the state. Job Search Assistance provides services to Title III eligibles in the nonmetropolitan areas of the state.

The Cone-Mills project in Hillsborough, North Carolina is part of a statewide Title III program operated by the Employment Security Commission in that state. Employment Security set up a temporary office in Hillsborough to staff the project.

The United Labor Agency project in Cleveland, Ohio is operated by a union social service agency in conjunction with the Teamsters Assistance Program, Inc. in that city.

The grant recipient for the Houston Community College-Texas Employment Commission project is, as the name suggests, a community college. In this case, the project is operated jointly with the Texas Employment Commission (the state Employment Service).

Exhibit 1-1
Case Study Projects

Project	Grant recipient	Eligible population	Primary services	Planned participants	Labor market unemployment rate (percent)
Cummins Engine Company Columbus, Indiana	Private company	Laid-off workers in a 3-county area	Assessment Job Club Classroom Training	850	12.2
GM-UAW Metropolitan Pontiac Retraining and Employment Program Pontiac, Michigan	Union-management	UAW members laid off from five General Motors plants	Assessment	2,280	20.2
Minnesota Iron Range Project Virginia, Minnesota	SDA	Laid-off iron miners and others in a 7-county area	Assessment Classroom Training Job Club Job Search Adult Basic Education Relocation	1,324	11.3
Job Search Assistance, Inc. Missouri	Nonprofit	Title III eligibles in the nonmetropolitan areas of the state	Assessment Job Club OJT	1,000	9.3–14.6
Cone-Mills Project Hillsborough, North Carolina	State Employment Security	Laid-off workers from a textile plant closing	Assessment Job Search Classroom Training OJT Adult Basic Education	400	3.1

United Labor Agency Cleveland, Ohio	Union	Title III eligibles in Cuyahoga County	Counseling & Assessment Job Search Classroom Training OJT	700	9.8
Houston Community College, Texas Employment Commission Houston, Texas	Community College	Laid-off workers from steel, oil, chemical, construction and food industries	Assessment Job Search Classroom Training	650	10.0
ASARCO Copper Smelter Project Tacoma, Washington	State Employment Security	Laid-off workers from the ASARCO Copper Smelter in Tacoma, Washington	Assessment Job Search Classroom Training OJT	300	8.4
Dane County Project Madison, Wisconsin	Community-Based Organization	Laid-off workers from closed foundry and other Title III eligibles	Assessment Job Search Classroom Training	218	4.8

The grant recipient and administrative entity for the ASARCO Copper Smelter project is the state Employment Security agency which set up and operates the ASARCO Resource Center. The Center has an advisory board made up of local, state and federal government officials, local and state Employment Security officials, an ASARCO official, unions, local social service agencies and the local Service Delivery Area director.

The Dane County project in Madison, Wisconsin has as the grant recipient Over 55 Employment Service, Inc., a community-based organization (CBO). The project is operated in conjunction with Project Fresh Start and the Employment and Training Association, two other CBOs in the county.

The grant recipients and program operators for the projects included in this volume, then essentially cover the range of possibilities available under Title III.

The primary eligible populations for these projects are also indicative of the range of possible coverage for Title III projects. This range includes: workers laid off as the result of a specific plant closing, as in the case of the Cone-Mills and ASARCO projects; laid-off workers from a number of firms within an area, as is the case in the Cummins Engine Company project; workers laid off from a particular industry in the case of the Minnesota Iron Range project; union members laid off from specific plants in an industry in the case of the Metropolitan Pontiac Retraining and Employment Program; workers laid off from several industries in an area in the case of the Houston Community College-Texas Employment Commission project; and any Title III eligible within the service area, as in the Cleveland, Ohio United Labor Agency project.

As indicated in exhibit 1-1, the range of primary services provided (i.e., the service provided to the largest numbers of the participants) includes: assessment only; assessment and job search; assessment, job search, and classroom training or on-the-job training; and, comprehensive services that emphasize long-term institutional training, OJT, adult basic education, and relocation.

As also indicated in exhibit 1-1, the unemployment rates in the areas in which the projects operate vary from 3.1 percent in Orange County, North Carolina to 20.2 percent in Pontiac, Michigan. However, the unemployment rate in the project area does not fully describe the labor market conditions in which the projects operate since it does not take into account the conditions in the larger labor market in which the project is located. A full description of the labor market conditions for each project is provided in the individual case studies.

The original intention was to select projects of roughly the same size. These projects were to have 500 to 1,000 planned participants. However, as exhibit 1-1 indicates, the range of actual size varies widely. There are several reasons for this. First, some projects actually served more people than planned. Second, in some cases, the project was not completed at the time of the observation on which the case study is based. Third, in some cases, the number of participants served indicated in exhibit 1-1 is greater than the number served with Title III funds. Finally, some exceptions were made to include projects that were important to capture the full range of some of the other program dimensions.

All of these projects were of particular interest along certain dimensions. They were also thought to be successful by the Title III staff at the state level, although, in some cases, with reservations. Finally, upon inquiry by the authors of the case studies, these projects appeared to be relatively successful in what they were attempting to do. In all cases, project staff were enthusiastic about their programs.

The following nine chapters (2 through 10) are the individual case studies. Chapter 11 contains our analysis of lessons learned from them that might be useful in understanding the Dislocated Worker Program under Title III of the Job Training Partnership Act and the kinds of services that might be of use to dislocated workers.

NOTES

1. Marc Bendick, "Government's Role in the Job Transitiions of America's Dislocated Workers," testimony at joint hearings on Technology and Employment, U.S. Congress, House Committee on the Budget, June 9, 1983.

2. Paul O. Flaim and Ellen Sehgal, "Displaced Workers of 1979-83: How Well Have They Fared?" *Monthly Labor Review*, June 1985, p. 3.

3. U.S. General Accounting Office, *Dislocated Workers: Extent of Business Closures, Layoffs, and the Public and Private Response* (GAO/HRD 86-116BR), July 1986, p. 11.

4. Office of Technology Assessment, *Technology and Structural Unemployment: Reemploying Displaced Adults*, Congress of the United States, Washington, D.C., p. 3.

5. U.S. Congress, *Job Training Partnership Act*, Public Law 97-300, October 13, 1982.

6. Wayne Turnage, Robert F. Cook, Ronna Cook and Associates, *The Organization of Title III of the Job Training Partnership Act in Fifty States*, Office of Research and Evaluation, Employment and Training Administration, U.S. Department of Labor, Washington, D.C., May 1984.

2
The Cummins Engine Company Dislocated Worker Project

Introduction

The grant recipient for this project is the Cummins Engine Company, a manufacturer of diesel truck engines located in Columbus, Indiana. The project was designed to provide job search and training to 850 dislocated workers laid off from Cummins and other firms within a three-county area in southern Indiana that surrounds Columbus. The Cummins Engine Company has manufacturing facilities in all three counties.

Background

In order to understand the context of this project, some background on the company and the community is appropriate. The Cummins Engine Company, the world's largest provider of diesel truck engines, was founded in Columbus in 1919. Although it has production facilities in a number of countries worldwide, the corporate headquarters are in Columbus, a city with a population slightly in excess of 30,000.

Two aspects of the Cummins Engine Company/Columbus, Indiana relationship are important to this context, one corporate and the other personal. First, the Cummins Engine Company is the largest employer in the three-county area. The company has a history of "progressive" management and, as a consequence, is often mentioned in the industrial relations literature. Independent unions represent its employees and wage rates are above those in this otherwise rural and nonunion area.

The personal side of this relationship is the former chairman of the Cummins Engine Company. The chairman, his family, and the Cummins Foundation have supported, directly and indirectly, the development of the Columbus environment. As an example, in the 1950s an agreement was reached between the Cummins Foundation and the school board by which, if the school board employed internationally known architects in the design of needed school buildings, the Foundation would provide the architectural fees. The local architectural tour now includes 47 public, religious, Cummins Engine, and other private facilities and works of sculpture. All of this is the result of corporate/individual citizen cooperation that emphasizes the development of the community.

The Local Labor Market

The local labor market (for the purposes of this project) comprises the following Indiana counties: Bartholomew, Jackson, and Jennings (all part of the larger Indiana Employment Security Division's Region 11). The City of Columbus, in Bartholomew County, is the largest urban center in the region. This area is part of a larger southern Indiana labor market, bounded by Cincinnati, Ohio; Louisville, Kentucky; and Indianapolis, Indiana, in which there is a substantial amount of commuting. Nearly 7,000 people commute to Bartholomew County, with nearly half coming from Jackson and Jennings Counties. The primary displacement in the region has occurred in these three counties.

When this project was being proposed (August 1983), the unemployment rates were 10.1, 12.2, and 12.2 percent for Bartholomew, Jackson, and Jennings counties, respectively. By the time the project started in January 1984, area unemployment was peaking for those counties at 11.2, 13.1, and 15.0 percent. Aided by a call-back at Cummins Engine Company in February-March 1984, the situation improved significantly. The June 1984 figures were 7.3 percent for Bartholomew, 9.0 percent for Jackson, and 9.5 percent for Jennings. This trend continued as the data for October 1984 show: Bartholomew, 6.3 percent; Jackson, 7.1 percent, and Jennings, 7.2 percent.

The most significant plant closing in the past two years (1984-85), at ITT-Thompson, left about 170 persons unemployed. Another firm, employing 60 persons, moved, and numerous small plant closings in the three-county area have left another 250 to 300 persons unemployed. Most significant to local employment have been layoffs, not closings. One firm, Golden Foundry (a supplier to Cummins), lost about 700 jobs. Three other firms account for another 250 jobs; Cummins still had approximately 1,500 workers on layoff as of the fall of 1985.

In spite of these and other negative examples, the local labor market has improved significantly in 1985, but still is not at prerecession levels. There are no major new areas or industries showing growth. The bulk of the improvement comes from rehiring. The largest growth area seems to be restaurants and some hotels. There is one small electronics/mechanical engineering firm that is increasing its business through development of new products, but this amounts to an increase of only about 35 jobs. Como, a plastics firm making styrofoam for the packaging of products, has increased employment by about 200 in the last 18 months. A food processing plant has increased employment by about 250, but these are on-call positions, not full-time employment.

Unionization is not very strong, although all the major plants have unions. Many workers are members of unaffiliated or local unions. There is not a strong prounion feeling in southern Indiana.

Local average wage rates are fairly high, principally because of Cummins, where starting pay for a janitor is $12.00 per hour. Arvin, a manufacturer of automotive exhaust systems, has an average pay scale of $7.00 to $8.50 per hour. Local wage rates are comparable to the state average manufacturing wage rate.

State Organization of Title III

The Indiana Office of Occupational Development is responsible for funding and program administration of both Title III and Title IIA. The executive director reports directly to the governor. Program emphasis is directed within the framework of economic development, the major thrust of the governor during his first term in office beginning in 1981.

Early in transition year 1984, funds were allocated on a project-by-project basis. In essence, these were experimental projects. The criteria were major closings and/or layoffs and the total economic impact on the community. Subsequently, a statewide allocation formula has been developed, but it has no direct bearing on this project.

The state had no fixed criteria as there were different circumstances in different communities. The economic impact may differ depending on the size of the layoff/closing relative to the size and industrial structure of the community. Eligibility criteria had to be justified in the proposed plans.

The state did not try to influence the mix of services. State staff admit that they ''really didn't know the best way'' of serving dislocated workers other than the feeling that there should not be a total reliance on job search given the industry-specific or rural setting of the projects.

Performance standards were negotiated with each project. Generally, there was a placement rate requirement of 50 to 70 percent; a cost per placement of less than $7,000; and requirements that the project not be overly duplicative of other services, and that it provide for coordination with other agencies and service operations in place.

A dislocated worker was defined as a worker who was laid off or terminated from a private business establishment and who was eligible for unemployment compensation, or who had exhausted unemployment compensation.

The Cummins Company came to the state to inquire about possible assistance for the area prior to the implementation of JTPA at the state level. Cummins saw a need in the area, not only for their own dislocated workers affected by world competition, but for those of other firms as well. The project was chosen as a pilot project among others in the state. The interest from the state appears to be that there was a need and that "something could be learned" working with a private firm—especially one with the favorable public relations image of Cummins.

Cummins staff prepared the grant proposal. Personnel from Cummins played a major role in identifying the problem and developing the proposal and the program concept. This included sending a team of people to examine the Downriver Community Conference Dislocated Worker Demonstration Project in Michigan. The Cummins program is operated under the auspices of an advisory board of 15 members. Five members are from Cummins, two from Golden Foundry, and the balance from the local Chamber of Commerce, the mayor's office, the local vocational education agency, the Employment Security office, and the Indiana Office of Occupational Development. Consequently, there is a strong private sector influence.

The Nature of the Project

Cummins Engine Company is the grant recipient. The company, in turn, subcontracted program operation to Brumbaugh, Scott, & Associates, a private consulting firm. Brumbaugh, Scott, & Associates are responsible for all day-to-day operations of the program except the job clubs. This activity was subcontracted to Charles W. Jaggers & Associates. Brumbaugh had experience with CETA and the human resource services field; Jaggers also had some CETA and human resource development experience.

A contract with Employment Security provides a wage history on each candidate coming into the program. In addition, a staff member from Employment Assistance Service, a subsidiary of Brumbaugh, Scott, & Associates, is provided office space in the Employment Security offices in the targeted areas. These individuals also have access to the master employer file in the Employment Security office.

Depending upon the interest of the candidates (they are not referred to as participants or clients) in skill upgrading or skill retraining, coordination and cooperation exists among all educational facilities within the region.

Candidates may work through the Area 11 Agency on Aging if they are 55 or older and desire to do so. This agency also operates a job club for candidates over the age of 55. Outside of the specific contracts, coordination depends on the nature, interests, and requirements of each candidate.

Two advisory board members from Cummins represent unions. There was no mention of any problems associated with the unions, nor was there any mention of strong union support. It must be remembered that the world headquarters of Cummins is located in a southern Indiana town of approximately 30,000 people.

No particular group is targeted for a service other than the previously stated criteria for eligibility. The initial contact must come from the individual (i.e., either walking through the door or sending in a postcard in response to newspaper advertisements). Participants come from many varied industries in the area. The major industries, in terms of percentage of participants, include Cummins (17 percent), Golden Foundry (3 percent), ITT (4 percent), and Stadler Packing (11 percent). One reason Stadler (a relatively small firm) accounts for such a high proportion of participants is that the workers were contacted within three weeks after the doors shut. In most other cases, the closings or layoffs took place up to two years before the program was started.

No particular firms or industries are targeted for placement. This is primarily because there is no single or small set of industries experiencing substantial growth in the area.

Services provided include assessment, job search skills, job club, classroom training, OJT, and placement. Placement is the ultimate goal. The project has been implemented as proposed except that the eligibility requirements can be satisfied by either residence in the three counties or being laid off from an industry in any of the three counties. This is in response to the recognized commuting patterns within the larger labor market area.

The Eligible Population

Workers targeted for the Cummins project were laid off from one of several sources in the Bartholomew, Jennings, and Jackson county area. They included: Cummins, 1,500; Golden Foundry, 700; ITT (North Vernon, factory closed), 170; Amoco Containers (Seymour, factory closed), 200; small factories closing in Jackson County, 200; Arvin, Cosco, and Reliance, 170; and, other small businesses (fast food, grocery stores, manufacturing firms, and small retail firms), 500. This comes to a total of 3,440. These estimates were prepared by the Employment Security Division.

Only workers who meet the following two general criteria were considered for enrollment:

(1) They have been or will be laid off or terminated from a private business establishment located in Bartholomew, Jackson, or Jennings County. (This was later modified to include residents of the three counties who may have been laid off from firms outside the counties.)

(2) They are or will be eligible for unemployment compensation, or have exhausted their unemployment compensation.

The specific selection criteria to determine who will enter the program are as follows. Eligible individuals:

- have experienced long spells of unemployment from a "base" job within the past four years;

- want to work in a high demand occupation and have skills or are trainable in those skills;

- attend and participate in pre-enrollment sessions;

- are unemployed from a "base" job in a business that has been closed;

- have no recall rights or seniority in their former job; and

- have no notification of being recalled to their former job.

The total project population included union and nonunion members as well as skilled and unskilled individuals. However, the bulk of the workers in the area are characterized as semiskilled to unskilled. Golden Foundry, which laid off 700 individuals, is noted for hiring the unskilled and uneducated. Prior wage levels were above the area average in some instances and below in others. Generally speaking, prior wage levels for project participants (aside from those at Cummins) are in line with the average in the area.

Program Services

Once an inquiry is received from a potential candidate, a half-day orientation workshop is scheduled. At this workshop, an overview of the program is explained along with the eligibility requirements. If the individual is interested, an application is filled out. All applications are checked through Employment Security to verify eligibility, i.e., employment and wage history.

At this point, a three-day workshop is scheduled for eligible applicants for group assessment and individual assessment counseling. The group assessment includes discussions on the job market, transferrable skills, self-evaluation and testing. Individual assessment includes a determination and negotiation of an appropriate service package.

The responsibility is always on the individual. It is up to the individual to make the initial contact, to attend the orientation, to attend the three-day workshop and, finally, to decide to enroll in one of the three basic alternatives. He or she must show motivation within the framework of "What do I want to do?" A basic philosophy of the program is that the candidate is a "well" being, with a history of being responsible, going to work, supporting a family, and paying taxes. With dislocation, he or she loses a meaningful routine of life. Therefore, the program is designed around the individual and his or her decisionmaking capabilities and not the individual molded into a specific program function. Exhibit 2-1 shows the decision points and flow through the program.

Exhibit 2-1
Cummins Project Participant Flow Chart

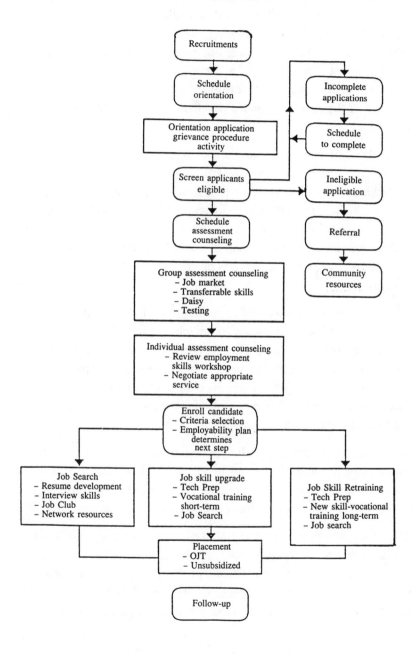

At the third (enrollment) stage, the candidate may decide whether or not to continue in the program. Even if the decision is to not continue, the individual still leaves with something in hand. The process of group and self-evaluation, including goal-setting, has been completed. The participant who decides not to continue has considerably more information about him or herself and the job environment than before contact was made. The reason for this procedure is that an original requirement of the Advisory Board was that ''everyone goes away with something.''

If the decision is to continue, the candidate will choose from one of three alternatives; job search, job skill upgrade, or job skill retraining. Job search includes resume development, interview skills development, joining a job club, and networking sources. Job skill upgrade is typically technical preparation or short-term vocational training. Job skill retraining also includes technical preparation and long-term new skill vocational training. The desired result is placement in OJT or unsubsidized employment.

At the end of December 1984, the distribution of participants was 20 in assessment, 108 in training, 263 in job club, and 26 in OJT. Given the voluntary nature of the program and participation in various program services, this represents a clear preference on the part of candidates for immediate job search over training. The program is candidate driven; that is, it depends upon the interest of the candidate after the group and individual assessment.

In terms of OJT, the general breakdown is approximately 50 percent in manufacturing and 50 percent in services. Manufacturing encompasses primarily production, tool and die, and job shop finish work. The service element ranges from office work to restaurant jobs.

Classroom training or skill upgrading is open. Anything available in the area, or outside it for that matter, can be selected by the candidate as long as it is related to the individual's preference and has potential for job placement. Four specific programs were established locally in the areas of nurse aid/home care, food service, industrial training, and business education. Enough participants were interested in each of these four areas that special programs were developed. Program length varies with the participant and his/her needs.

Counseling is an important component of the total program. The emphasis is primarily on job search skills. This is true regardless of whether the participant moves directly into job search and the job club or selects job skill upgrade or job skill retraining.

Counseling with regard to wage level expectations begins as soon as a potential participant comes through the door. All aspects of group and individual assessment are couched in the framework of the reality of the job market compared to the particular interests and reasonable salary expectations of each candidate. Individuals who offer information or are identified as having other unemployment-related problems (e.g., financial or psychological) are referred to other appropriate agencies.

Program Participants

Most participants come from manufacturing industries in production work. There are exceptions including such occupations as food service, truck drivers, and employees of a car dealership, a cocktail lounge, a remodeling business, an engineering firm, and the Navy. No groups are given priority or selected for specific program services. Any individual meeting the eligibility requirements and with the interest and desire to undertake the program is enrolled. The characteristics of the participants are shown in table 2-1.

Job placement takes a dual approach: (1) individual job search and networking, and (2) industrial representatives on the program staff looking for jobs to match to candidates and passing on discovered job openings. Much of the emphasis is on individual job search through the job clubs. The industrial representatives are responsive to the candidates, their interests and requirements. If the representatives discover openings, they are automatically passed on. There are a few instances of a prior agreement with an employer to hire a candidate and to provide specific training to that candidate.

Table 2-1
Enrollment and Participant Characteristics
for Calendar Year 1984, Selected Characteristics

Selected characteristics	Number	Percent
Total participants	708	
Total terminations	294	
Entered employment	245	83
Other positive terminations	49	17
Other terminations	—	—
Sex		
Male	201	68
Female	93	32
Age		
14–15	—	—
16–19	2	1
20–21	11	4
22–44	210	71
45–54	48	16
55 and over	23	8
Education		
School dropout	89	30
Student (H.S. or less)		
High school graduate or more	205	70
Race		
White	284	97
Black	7	2
Hispanic	2	1
Native American	1	*
Asian		
Employment barriers		
Limited English	1	*
Handicapped	1	*
Offender	25	9
Other		
Benefit recipiency		
U.I. claimant	145	49
U.I. exhaustee	149	51
Public assistance	51	17
AFDC	5	2
Youth AFDC	—	—
Labor force status (prior 26 weeks)		
Unemployed 1–14 weeks	110	37
Unemployed 15 or more weeks	184	63
Not in labor force	—	—

*Less than .5 percent.

Candidates 55 or older have the option to participate in the Area 11 Agency on Aging program. Other than those who choose this option, the placement process does not significantly differ for particular groups or by program activity.

Program Outcomes

The process appears to be relatively successful in that 245 placements have resulted from 294 total terminations (an 83 percent placement rate). Again, the program is candidate-driven and no particular firms/organizations are targeted for placement. Relocation is an almost insignificant part of the placement process.

Performance standards were incorporated as goals, rather than as terms of the contract, with a target of 850 enrolled and 440 placed. Performance levels were included in programs established subsequent to the Cummins project.

Aside from the 83 percent placement rate of terminees mentioned above, the calculated cost per placement to date is $3,732. Both the placement rate and the cost per placement figures may be biased upward by the fact that only 294 of the 708 people in the program have been terminated. The program was to continue to operate through June 1985.

The average wage on the "base" job (the one from which the candidate was originally laid off) for those terminated was $8.07 per hour. The average wage of those placed is $5.60 per hour. This represents a 69 percent wage replacement ratio.

Exhibit 2-2 shows the distributions of occupations entered by those placed at termination.

Overall Assessment

No real problems came to light during the review of this project. However, a few points of interest are worth emphasizing.

Exhibit 2-2
Cummins Placements, Occupations Entered
(Percentage distribution)

	Percent
Executive, administrative, and managerial occupations	6
Engineers, surveyors, and architects	6
Natural scientists and mathematicians	6
Social scientists, social workers, religious workers, lawyers	6
Teachers, librarians, counselors	6
Health diagnosing and treatment practitioners	6
Registered nurses, pharmacists, dietitians, therapists, etc.	6
Writers, artists, entertainers, athletes	6
Health technologists and technicians	6
Technologists and technicians, except health	6
Marketing and sales occupations	11
Administrative support occupations, including clerical	7
Service occupations	16
Agricultural, forestry, and fishing occupations	1
Mechanics and repairers	7
Construction and extractive occupations	1
Precision production occupations	18
Production working occupations	18
Transportation and material moving occupations	8
Handlers, equipment cleaners, helpers, and laborers	8
Miscellaneous occupations	4

During the initial stages of the project, it appeared that the state did not know exactly what to expect of a project funded to a private entity. In some ways, it appears the state expected much more than it got, but didn't know explicitly what it wanted.

There was some infighting among the local SDA and the PIC, local training organizations, and Cummins and the private consultant retained to operate the program. The problem appears to be securing turf. Some of the actors were from CETA backgrounds and the CETA philosophy was evident. This did not go over well with the Cummins project people who saw their "candidates" as quite different from the CETA—JTPA Title IIA "clients."

There was also some misunderstanding and/or misinformation early on as to who was going to handle the day-to-day operation of the program. The fact that Cummins did not "run" the program caused some consternation at the state level. The fact that a private consulting firm did run the program caused even more.

Apparently, based on past history, the state expected Cummins to actually operate the program "with its usual public relations flair." The Cummins executives and the advisory board saw the problem as a community problem and wanted the project set up as a community project outside of Cummins. In fact, the original project proposal indicated that program operations would be subcontracted.

A Cummins representative stated that "we probably wouldn't do it again knowing what we do now." There may be some insight here in terms of the potential for public/private partnerships in programs of this nature. On the one hand, there is the public sector which is process-oriented and, on the other, the private sector (in this case an international corporation) which is results-oriented. The latter is interested in getting in, getting it done, and getting out. The former more oriented to regulations, reports, meetings, and processes.

It was recognized that the eligible population for the project differed from those eligible for Title IIA. There was also recognition of the cultural background associated with a long-time southern Indiana resident. The project was well designed for the local area and the local population.

The self-selection process of candidates and the timing of the program may have limited its total potential impact. Many individuals had been laid off for some time before the project was in place. Some of these people had found their own employment, moved, or given up and left the labor force before assistance was available.

Given the nature of the local economic base, the local employment scene and the associated problems of layoffs and plant closings, the program seems to be adequate to the problem. It would not be socially or politically feasible to target a specific firm or industry for a dislocated worker program in this region. It would also not be operationally feasible to target specific industries or occupations for retraining and re-employment. The economic base is neither that large nor that diverse.

3
The GM-UAW Metropolitan Pontiac Retraining and Employment Program (PREP)

Introduction

The Metropolitan Pontiac Retraining and Employment Program (PREP) is a joint union-management (GM-UAW) project. It was designed to provide assessment, job search, and training to 13,000 dislocated United Auto Worker members in the Pontiac, Michigan area who had been laid off from five General Motors plants. The project was originally funded out of fiscal year 1983 and transition year 1984 state Title III funds.

The Origin of the Project

The City of Pontiac, Michigan lies about 15 miles northwest of the city center of Detroit. Downtown Detroit is surrounded by white, prosperous suburbs on both the north and west sides. The Detroit SMSA and the labor market area consist of five counties arrayed in roughly a semicircle around downtown Detroit. The other part of the circle is Windsor, Ontario. Oakland County is the northwest quadrant of this labor market area and Pontiac constitutes a satellite center within the larger labor market.

Pontiac and Oakland County represent a microcosm of the Greater Detroit area in the sense that the City of Pontiac is heavily black and very depressed, and it is surrounded in turn by very prosperous, white suburbs. This can be clearly seen in the unemployment rates for the relevant areas.

In 1982 and 1983, the entire Detroit area labor market was depressed due to the cyclical decline in the auto industry. The annual average unemployment rate in 1982 was 15.9 percent in Detroit, and in 1983 it was 14.6 percent. The City of Pontiac's annual average unemployment rate for 1982 was an astronomical 28.2 percent. This was due to a heavy concentration of auto installations in the Pontiac area. In July of 1984, when the total unemployment rate for the State of Michigan stood at 11.3 percent, the Detroit SMSA unemployment rate was 11.4 percent and the Oakland County unemployment rate was 10.2 percent. The City of Pontiac in July of 1984 suffered an unemployment rate of 20.2 percent, while the rates in such suburban communities as Farmington Hills, Royal Oak City and Southfield hovered around 8 percent. Labor market distress in Pontiac is worsened by the contrast to the prospering high tech- and service industry-oriented suburbs nearby. Pontiac is a pocket of black poverty in the midst of one of the highest income areas in the Midwest.

The general condition of the Pontiac labor market in the last few years has reflected large scale unemployment in the auto industry with up to 40 percent of production workers on indefinite layoff. At the same time, robotics and CAD/CAM suppliers are moving into the Southfield and Farmington Hills area to cater to the demand for such capital goods from the auto industry. This has led to an alteration in the job outlook for both blue-collar and white-collar workers. There is more demand than ever for highly skilled and highly specialized sales and service workers while there has been less and less demand for unskilled and semiskilled manufacturing workers. However, the last 12 months prior to this study in the fall of 1985 have shown significant improvement in employment, even within the manufacturing establishments, as the auto industry has recovered to more normal employment levels.

Among the many plant closings in the Pontiac area were two of the plants from which the eligible population for this project was drawn.

A Fisher Body plant in Pontiac has closed permanently. As will be discussed later, this is balanced in the current situation by the opening of the new General Motors plant within the City of Pontiac. In addition, a plant that was thought to have been closed permanently, Pontiac Plant 8, is now being refitted for G-Car production and will be hiring some 2,500 workers over the next few months.

State Organization of Title III

The Governor's Office for Job Training (GOJT) is the organizational unit responsible for Title III. It was created in response to JTPA. This office is part of the governor's executive staff, and the director of the Governor's Office for Job Training has direct access to the governor. The Bureau of Employment and Economic Development (BEED) in the Michigan Department of Labor has responsibility for contract administration, including the data reporting requirements imposed by the Act. This agency is also responsible for administering the Title IIA program in the State of Michigan.

This description makes the situation sound somewhat more regular than it actually is, however. The Governor's Office for Job Training oversees contract performance in the areas of retraining and job creation. The BEED's responsibility is primarily on the fiscal management side. There are some obvious problems inherent in this division of responsibilities, which represents the outcome of an earlier dispute over control of JTPA within state government. With the recent turnover of the directors of both the Governor's Office for Job Training and the Michigan Department of Labor, it is anticipated that further rationalization of this organizational structure may occur in the near future.

There is no single focus to the Michigan Title III program. In general, the Michigan Job Training Coordinating Council (MJTCC) expressed an intense interest in the economic development goals of the state and set aside 25 percent of Title III funding for that purpose. However, it is also clear that the existing political and economic realities and the historic importance of the auto industry in the State of Michigan shaped the decisions of the MJTCC and GOJT.

In the first round of decisions for FY 1983 and transition year 1984 funds, the auto industry had a preferred position. Just over 50 percent of all Title III allocations for the first year went to three auto projects ($5.74 million out of a total of $10.98 million). The Chrysler Learning Project received $1.5 million against $3.38 million in matching funds to retrain 500 displaced Chrysler workers. The UAW-Ford National Development and Training Center received $1.85 million against a $1.6 million match to retrain 860 displaced Ford workers. The Pontiac GM-UAW PREP project received $2.39 million against $2.51 million in match to retrain 2,280 dislocated GM employees.

The Governor's Office for Job Training used an RFP process to distribute the Title III resources. This was not a regular procedure since this was a new agency and there was considerable delay in setting policies. In addition, the process was held up by the internal disputes between the new agency and the Michigan Department of Labor as to the roles each was to play in administering JTPA funds in the state. The result was that GOJT was overwhelmed with proposals before it ever actually released an RFP.

No funds were allocated on a formula basis; however, the auto industry obligations could be considered an informal set-aside for Michigan's largest industry which was in desperate trouble at that time. The Title III Subcommittee of MJTCC indicated in August 1983, that a "substantial majority" of the 75 percent of Title III funds remaining after the economic development priorities were satisfied would be available for joint and/or large management-labor Dislocated Worker Programs.

The original policy statement for Title III indicates that the state did not establish eligibility criteria beyond those in the Act. The state did establish priorities for funding; leveraged proposals, and those which included training for specific jobs with specific employers requiring specific skills were given the highest priorities. Further, both geographic and industrial diversity was sought.

There is no indication that the state tried to influence the mix of services for its Title III programs. Rather, the competitive RFP process was designed to help illuminate the needs of displaced workers in the state and the GOJT saw its task as choosing the winners from the competition. The governor's special services plan did not impose any service requirements on Title III operators.

The state does maintain performance standards for Title III projects. The overall goal is an entered employment rate of 55 percent, adjusted according to the expectations in the particular labor markets faced by the clients of the various projects. However, this does not constitute performance-based contracting and the standards are treated as goals rather than requirements.

The Nature of the Project

The GM-UAW Metropolitan Pontiac Retraining and Employment Program (PREP) is the recipient organization of the Title III grant. This is a joint labor-management effort with two equal co-directors, one from each organization. For the most part, PREP runs the program on its own. Some of the program has been subcontracted, but not a major share. As it was created for this purpose in 1983, PREP had no previous experience in operating employment and training programs. However, with a first year budget of $4.7 million, it had no trouble hiring people with the requisite experience. It also hired some displaced auto workers for the PREP staff.

There are significant linkages between this project and other components of the employment and training system but this largely reflects the size of the PREP program. Nonfinancial agreements exist with the Michigan Employment Security Commission, the Department of Social Services, the United Way, the local Vocational Rehabiitation Office, and the two PICs in the area. For the most part, such agreements represent the outreach efforts by PREP to locate and inform eligible UAW members of its existence.

Virtually all local training organizations are in intermittent contact with the PREP personnel; this is because they are trying to tap into the PREP funding sources. PREP takes a careful approach to these initiatives,as it is unwilling to be seen as the source of handouts. The various employment and training programs are not coordinated at this point because they are serving different populations with different needs and with different objectives in mind.

For the purposes of the Pontiac Retraining and Employment Program, a dislocated worker was defined as a UAW member with contractual recall rights (90 days minimum employment) on layoff from one of five General Motors plants in the Pontiac area. As of the summer of 1983, this involved a potential eligible population of 13,000 displaced workers. At the beginning of the PREP program, it was anticipated that it would take three years to retrain and place all these auto workers.

The prior wage levels of the UAW members were above the average in the local economy. However, Pontiac is basically a GM town, so the wages were typical for UAW members. Most of the laid-off UAW members would be in the semiskilled category. Some of those with the least seniority who were included in the earliest layoffs could be regarded as unskilled. There would be few, it any, skilled trades workers among those laid off by GM who would not have been recalled by the summer of 1983.

When this program began in the summer of 1983, it was generally accepted that UAW members, some of whom had been laid off since late 1979, were permanently displaced from their jobs in the auto industry. The 1982 GM-UAW national contract agreement set up a fund for the retraining of such workers with an employer contribution of 5 cents for every hour worked by UAW members (the ''Nickel Fund''). The GM-UAW PREP project was funded jointly by this Nickel Fund and by the GOJT allocation of JTPA Title III funds. Roughly half the total funding of $4.7 million was expected to come from each source. Thus, the joint funding from the GM-UAW contract and the State of Michigan's Title III allocation seemed to provide the opportunity for retraining some of those 13,000 displaced auto workers for other employment.

Even before state funding was finalized, a retraining program was begun for auto workers in Pontiac to be trained as industrial sewing machine operators for a GM trim plant in Grand Rapids. The training was subcontracted out and a total of 260 auto workers were eventually placed in the Grand Rapids facility. Since the contract was not yet finalized with GOJT, the workers were required to pay their own relocation costs in Grand Rapids. Reports indicate that a good deal of hardship resulted, but the feeling was that these auto workers had no future in Pontiac and the GM-UAW contract did not allow expenditures for relocation. The Pontiac workers who relocated to Grand Rapids were required to relinquish all recall rights to their original jobs. Base pay in Grand Rapids was $9.63/hour, but still only one prospect in six was willing to relocate.

Because of the continuing delays in finalizing a JTPA Title III contract in Lansing, the PREP project began to go more slowly in planning retaining and reemployment efforts. At the same time, the fortunes of GM, and Pontiac in particular, picked up remarkably. The result was that the supposedly displaced workers were being recalled by GM more rapidly than they could be trained for alternative employment. In addition, since everyone understood that the best alternative employment might require wage sacrifices of one-third or more compared to their former auto industry jobs, few displaced workers were anxious to volunteer for retraining. In the final analysis, the delays in Lansing may have prevented attempts to retrain workers who, it turned out, were shortly to be recalled to their old jobs.

Changing Project Direction

When this observation of the PREP project took place in November 1984, they were testing and evaluating the last of the 13,000 project eligible laid-off auto workers in Pontiac. These workers were being prepared to return to work early in 1985 at the refurbished Pontiac G-Car plant. They had been laid off exactly five years previously in

November 1979 in the earliest wave of auto layoffs. Some had only a few months GM experience, as they were a part of the employment buildup in the auto industry in 1978 and early 1979. While this could not have been anticipated in the summer of 1983, it is nevertheless the case that the recovery of GM sales and the opening of two new Pontiac Motor Division plants in Pontiac (the Fiero plant and the G-Car plant) plus the GMAD-ORION plant nearby, served to effectively absorb the displaced auto workers in a relatively short period of time.

The current program, as it relates to the 2,500 G-Car employees, can be regarded as illustrative of the PREP mission at this point in time. The former auto workers are being assessed, tested, and re-enrolled as GM employees at the PREP facility. Those who require very basic remedial education are being targeted for a new program at the Wisner School which will provide remedial education required to make them functional in the new Pontiac plants upon their return.

The remainder are being slotted into a three-week G-Car orientation program at the Wever School facility, which is maintained by PREP. This is not a traditional skill training program, but an attempt to change the attitudes of both supervisors and assembly workers. The purpose is to mold the "new auto worker," one appropriate to a more participative and cooperative labor-management environment. The trainees are being exposed to statistical process control and other quality control concepts but the primary objective of the training is to produce a new winning attitude among the employees of the Pontiac Motor Division. PREP is performing these services under a $1.5 million contract with the Pontiac Motor Division. Some enrollees and some services can be funded with Title III money, but most of the activity is funded privately.

The GM-UAW PREP project was really never fully implemented as proposed because of the rapidly changing employment situation described earlier. The project expected to conduct skill training and outplacement services for displaced auto workers and instead ended up being an intake and assessment service for recalled auto workers. This accounts for a placement rate of 93 percent overall with very low cost per entered employment. On the other hand, it also presents a problematical future for PREP itself, which is exploring two different future modes. The first is reflected in the expansion of the eligible population to the statewide base of displaced auto workers. This would give PREP the possibility of reaching out to Flint, Saginaw, or Detroit to channel displaced auto workers in those sites into GM or other jobs. It also is possible that PREP will develop a mission within Pontiac Motor Division as the locus of intake, assessment, training, and retraining for Pontiac's workers.

The only adjustment in the population to be served concerns the treatment of the more senior and the less senior UAW members. Originally, the most senior GM employees were targeted for services. But as the recalls overwhelmed the ability of the project to prepare people, the focus eventually switched to the least senior. The concept was to move to the end of the recall list to find those auto workers with the least chance of returning to their former jobs.

The private sector involvement in the PREP program is dominant. While the original budget was roughly half private money, of the funds expended through October 31, 1984 only about 28 percent are public monies with roughly 72 percent being GM-UAW nickel-per-hour contract funds. In fact, this is one of the major complications of the Pontiac program since there are two funding sources and two bookkeeping systems, but really one integrated program. Charges are allocated according to the eligibility of the particular dislocated worker being treated and according to the program activity.

The PREP program is definitely a joint union-management program. The co-directors represent the two constituencies and the board of directors of PREP is divided equally between the company and the union. The Nickel Fund itself was an item negotiated between the union and the company in the 1982 contract.

Service Provided

The service sequence has varied with the needs of the individuals and to some degree the needs of the company. There have been three broad types of treatment: the original industrial sewing training group (n=342), an employability skills training group (n=75) for those who did not want to return to GM, and the OJT group (n=1,749) representing those who have been recalled to GM facilities. Since the major emphasis of the program to date has been on this last group, that service plan will be described.

The PREP program for the Pontiac G-Car recalls is as follows. The first major task is to locate the prospective dislocated workers. These people have been laid off for almost five years and locating them is by no means easy. As an example, in the Grand Rapids sewing machine project, letters were sent to 1,800 UAW members, of whom 700 (39 percent) could not be located.

Second in the sequence are two one-day sessions involving intake, assessment, and feedback to the clients. Prospective enrollees are assessed for eligibility for JTPA assistance under Title III, and the Michigan Occupational Data Analysis System is administered to determine their skill level. The Test of Adult Basic Education is also administered. It is interesting that the GM-UAW PREP project will be able, as a result of the testing, to help the company design training projects appropriate to the general skill level of the workers. This may not be possible in the absence of the joint union-management administration of this program. One week later, enrollees return to get the results of the testing and to be assigned to treatment groups. Counseling is also administered at this time to motivate the clients to consider their worklife preferences.

Stage three is the orientation program mentioned earlier. Some workers are slotted for basic remedial education classes at the Wisner School but the bulk of them go directly to the three-week orientation in the G-Car program at the Wever School. The emphasis is on team building, learning to trust your fellow workers, and understanding the importance of a quality product (a ''world class'' car). Workers coming out of this program understand that their personal prosperity is tied to the success of the product in the marketplace.

The services are quite basic. The training at the Wever School is classified as OJT, but is primarily an orientation to the new product and the new attitude required of Pontiac Motor Division employees. The remedial classroom training had not yet commenced at the time of this observation. Basic reading and arithmetic are planned. The various classes of clients throughout the first year of operation of the Wever School orientation program received training varying from three to five weeks in length. At the time of the observation, the standard was a three-week stint. The question of specific skill training is made much more difficult because of the simplicity of the job classifications in the new General Motors plants. There are two blue-collar job classifications at the GMAD-ORION plant and three at the Pontiac Fiero plant. One part of the new General Motors strategy is to eliminate the former complex and rigid job hierarchy within the plant.

The PREP project also has a two-week employability skills component with an optional extension to three weeks. This component is for those who prefer not to return to GM. The first week involves resume preparation, coping skills, etc., while the second week involves job search skills. However, virtually all the current clients are being recalled to jobs with General Motors, so it is not clear which clients will be going through the employability skills program in the future. Basically, this element of the PREP program has been undermined by the recall to employment for these clients.

Characteristics of Participants

As indicated earlier, the participants in the PREP program are former General Motors employees and UAW members. For the most part, they held assembler jobs in the auto plants. Eligibile participants were enrolled according to seniority lists until it became clear that most unemployed auto workers in Pontiac would be reemployed by the G-Car project. Then the priority was switched to those who were about to fall off the five-year recall cliff and lose all rights as former General Motors employees. Individuals without the requisite level of reading and arithmetic skills are slotted for additional training but will be recalled to the plants as well.

Table 3-1
Characteristics of Participants in the GM-UAW Metropolitan Pontiac Retraining and Employment Program through October 30, 1984

Characteristic	Number	Percent
Total	2,189	
Sex		
Male	1,493	68
Female	696	32
Age		
Youth (under 22)	12	1
Adult	2,177	99
Race		
White	1,482	68
Black	567	26
American Indian	21	1
Asian	13	1
Hispanic	106	5
Employment barriers		
Veteran	139	6
Handicapped	15	1
Receiving assistance		
UI recipient	37	2
Welfare recipient	248	11

These displaced GM workers are an entirely different population from those eligible for Title IIA. They are older, more male, less minority, and much less likely to be UI recipients at the time of enrollment. The latter is due to length of layoff as most are UI exhaustees. Table 3-1 shows the client characteristics reported from the start of the project in September 1983 through the end of October 1984. These characteristics reflect the fact that these are experienced workers who had held good jobs in the primary labor market at some point in the past.

Program Outcomes

As described above, the participants are being placed back into the General Motors plants in Pontiac, so this arrangement is most similar to prior agreements with particular employers to hire program participants. But in fact, this program goes far beyond that. In a real sense, the PREP program is a location, assessment, and reorientation program operating at the request of and for the benefit of a private employer. The bulk of the money expended to date on the program has also come from the coffers of that private employer. In a narrow sense, the program is extremely effective, since low cost and high placement rates have been secured. However, it must be pointed out that the challenge has not been anything like what was expected. While all anticipated that these GM-UAW workers had been permanently displaced, in fact it turned out they had not. The challenge for PREP has been to carve out a new mission for the organization in the face of a vanishing clientele.

Interestingly, relocation expenses are not allowed in the GM-UAW contract for workers who have lost their seniority recall rights. Thus, Nickel Fund money cannot be used for these purposes. One of the possible missions for the PREP program in the future is to act as the relocation allowance grantor for the General Motors employees who do need to be relocated to other plants. The fact that all Pontiac UAW members who could be located have gone back to work may end up benefiting GM employees in other sites where all workers have not been so lucky.

Wage data at original layoff were not available on an individual basis. The average wage at placement is the GM entry wage of $8.50 to $9.00 per hour, so there is probably little or no wage loss. Costs per placement are estimated at $900 to $1,000. To date, the overall placement rate is 93 percent.

However, as discussed earlier, the placements are back into General Motors facilities into the same kinds of jobs from which these workers were laid off four or five years earlier. The project has a state-imposed entered employment rate standard of 70 percent. There is also a clear recognition that performance will play a role in the allocation of funds for the next fiscal year.

Overall Assessment

The Pontiac GM-UAW PREP project experience raises some very difficult policy issues that occur in Displaced Worker Programs. The ultimate issue is, "When is a worker on layoff from a cyclical industry truly displaced?" When this project began operation in September of 1983, very few observers believed that the UAW members who had been on layoff in Pontiac for three to four years would ever return to their jobs. That was the reason for the JTPA Title III award in the first place.

As it turned out, however, most of those workers *were* recalled. With the benefit of perfect hindsight, it is now apparent that the displaced auto workers were not permanently displaced, but were simply on longer term cyclical layoff than had been experienced in the auto industry previously. Whether this is a new cyclical pattern or an historical anomaly will not be known for many years. The policy question is "What is the optimal intervention strategy for workers in this situation?"

Retraining is the usual response, but it is probably not realistic to try to retrain auto workers to a point where they can attain equivalent earnings in other sectors of the economy. It would not be cost effective to try to do so. There is also some question whether it makes sense to retrain laid-off auto workers for other jobs and then in a year or two train entirely new auto workers when employment returns to former levels. Thus, one might argue that the most appropriate intervention for many of these workers may have been more generous income maintenance programs (either public or private) to tide them over longer layoff periods. But, then, how are the workers (or policymakers) to decide when it is time to give up and look for some other opportunity?

There are two lessons to be learned from this experience. The first is that we should make every effort to be sure that displaced workers *are,* in fact, displaced and they themselves understand that they are displaced. It is possible that some of the GM workers had a more accurate assessment of their future recall chances than did employment and training authorities. This is not to denigrate the efforts of those who were trying to assist them. It is not an easy matter to determine when a worker is truly displaced. But it is also not easy to retrain workers for lower wage jobs when they believe they still might be recalled.

The second lesson is that the attitude of the displaced worker may be the most important factor of all. Some displaced auto workers chose to leave the industry, never to return, rather than wait to be recalled. With each severe cyclical employment drop, some workers lose heart and decide a more certain income stream, even though more modest, may be a better strategy. It seems clear that there could be a need for a program to retrain and place such "volunteers." Moreover, such a program should be much more individually oriented. The individual should be assisted in choosing training appropriate to his or her situation without attempting to enforce class-size or larger treatment groups.

While it is easy to second guess a program design after completion, it does appear that there were two different kinds of displaced workers in Pontiac. One group simply wanted income maintenance to keep body and soul together until the inevitable (in their mind) recall to their old jobs. The other group, who wanted to leave the area or the industry, probably did not receive assistance in time and made their own way as best they could. This suggests the necessity for a program with a broader focus to accommodate the diverse needs of the participants.

It is to the considerable credit of the PREP program operators that they did not persist with their original design in the face of a rapidly changing world. While they may have been assisted by resistance on the part of the clients, they nonetheless showed a clear orientation to the best interests of both General Motors and the UAW members by declining to engage in training simply for the sake of spending the funds.

Over a period of six months or so, the program found a new need under the General Motors umbrella and reoriented itself to providing the workers with the attitudes required to help build the new General Motors. The fact that this is being done under the aegis of a joint union-management program is probably critical to its ultimate success. Clearly, the typical production worker in the auto industry does not trust the company to look after his interests. But when the company and the union together fund a program that urges him to come back to work with a fresh new approach, tremendous changes in attitude are possible.

The enthusiasm and commitment of the instructors at the Wever School are inescapable testament to this kind of new beginning in the auto industry. Their stories illustrate that at least some, and perhaps a majority, of participants in the PREP project are going back to work with new attitudes and a new approach to the acquisition of new skills in the plant.

The testing and assessment being done at PREP could prove invaluable in designing effective training programs for employees in the plant after recall. It is no exaggeration to say that this kind of information could not have been accumulated on an experienced unionized labor force by the company acting on its own. Once again the joint union-management administration emerges as the key element to the success of the program.

The original contract for the PREP project was written to run from September 1983 through the end of November 1984. It has been extended twice and now will run through the end of March 1985. At the time of this observation in mid-November 1984, only about 23 percent of the Title III allocation had been expended. (Nearly 60 percent of GM-UAW Nickel Funds had been spent, however.) With pressure exerted from the U.S. Department of Labor on the State of Michigan to ensure that these monies are expended in a timely fashion, it is possible that the contract will not be renewed. In the sense of serving the needs of the original Pontiac displaced workers, this is probably appropriate. The company and the union may continue funding this program out of their own funds in any event. If this scenario develops, the GM-UAW PREP project may become one of the few JTPA Title III projects to become a permanent self-sustaining activity in the private sector.

4
The Minnesota Iron Range Dislocated Worker Project

Introduction

The Iron Range dislocated worker project operates in a seven-county Service Delivery Area (SDA) in northeastern Minnesota, known as the Arrowhead Region, which surrounds, but does not include, the City of Duluth. The area includes the Mesabi Iron Range, a series of open pit taconite mines that supply iron ore to the domestic steel industry located in the Great Lakes region. The project, operated by the Northeast Minnesota Office of Job Training was designed to provide job search, OJT, classroom training, and relocation assistance to 900 individuals from the mines and related industries during the transition year.

The Local Labor Market

Dislocated workers on the Iron Range are predominately miners who have been laid off as a result of reduced demand for steel, and consequently for taconite. However, given the severe economic conditions faced on the Range, the area's unemployed include many from mining-related industries, as well as from basic industries whose business has suffered over the past five years.

With the exception of excluding Duluth, the boundaries of SDA3 essentially define the northeast Minnesota labor market (see figure 4-1). The primary justification used to designate the City of Duluth as a separate SDA from the rest of the region is that it has a distinct labor market, linked more with Superior, Wisconsin than SDA3, although

47

overall conditions are not appreciably better in Duluth than in the rest
of the region.

Figure 4-1
SDA Boundaries of Northeast Minnesota

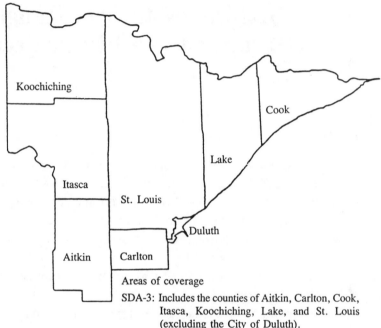

Areas of coverage
SDA-3: Includes the counties of Aitkin, Carlton, Cook,
Itasca, Koochiching, Lake, and St. Louis
(excluding the City of Duluth).

SD-4: The City of Duluth.

As can be seen in table 4-1, the unemployment trend for the region
is downward in 1984, reversing the patterns since 1979 (except during
1981). Still, the six-month average for the first half of 1984 was 14
percent, so the region remains depressed relative to the rest of the state
and the nation. The June 1984 unemployment rate for the region was
11.3 percent compared to 7 percent nationally and 6.2 percent for all
of Minnesota. While official statistics were not yet available at this
writing, there have been some sizable recent layoffs that have undoubted-
ly increased unemployment, or at best, halted its decline. A significant
part of the reduced unemployment has been the result of a declining
labor force, a pattern which is likely to continue.

Table 4-1
Labor Force Statistics for Northeast Minnesota
1972-1983 (annual averages) and 1984 (monthly averages)

Year/month	Labor force			Unemployment rate
	Total	Employed	Unemployed	
1972	86,801	80,906	5,895	6.8
1973	87,074	80,945	6,220	7.2
1974	87,143	81,441	5,702	6.5
1975	90,566	83,370	7,196	7.9
1976	93,678	85,695	7,983	8.5
1977	95,670	87,078	8,592	9.0
1978	102,187	96,215	5,972	5.8
1979	105,800	98,768	7,032	6.6
1980	108,849	96,172	12,677	11.6
1981	106,732	96,560	10,172	9.5
1982	110,437	89,288	21,149	19.2
1983	106,830	85,780	21,050	19.7
1984				
January	102,915	83,934	18,891	18.4
February	98,611	83,884	14,727	14.9
March	98,610	84,880	13,730	13.9
April	100,800	86,928	13,872	13.8
May	102,332	90,212	12,120	11.8
June	104,208	92,473	11,735	11.3

SOURCE: Minnesota Department of Economic Security. Data pertains to SDA3.

The biggest single problem for the region has been the decline of the taconite industry, with both mining and related construction employment falling by over 50 percent from 1979 peak levels (see table 4-2). Because these industries provide the highest wages in the area, their decline has had significant effects on the overall economy of the region.

Mining on the Mesabi Iron Range began around the turn of the century. The quality of the ore, its easy accessibility, and a ready-made harbor in Duluth led to a rapid development along the entire Range. The major cities in the region (aside from Duluth), i.e., Hibbing, Chisholm, Virginia, Eveleth, Babbitt, and Ely, grew up on the edge of the mines. Many, in fact, have been loaded on railroad cars and moved one or more times as the mines expanded. Related industries attracted by the iron ore, including a steel mill and several foundries (all since closed) moved in quickly, and development of the Duluth-Superior harbor turned it into the shipping center for grain from the northern Midwest. The economy of the region appears to have reached its peak in the early 1920s, as evidenced by the dates on major buildings in Duluth and throughout the Range and the architecture of the mansions of the iron and railroad barons along the north shore of Lake Superior.

Table 4-2
Covered Employment by Industry, 1978-1983
(annual averages) for SDA3

	1983	1982	1981	1980	1979	1978
Covered employment	59,580	61,367	69,533	70,785	75,174	72,990
Mining	7,120	8,903	13,706	13,962	15,545	13,694
Construction	2,053	2,361	2,681	3,342	5,318	5,368
Manufacturing	8,529	8,611	9,168	9,317	10,284	10,370
Transportation, common, public utility	2,245	2,193	2,334	2,237	2,288	2,174
Trade	13,929	14,184	15,078	15,416	15,658	14,909
Finance, insurance, real estate	1,807	1,956	2,006	1,981	1,949	1,825
Services & miscellaneous	10,980	10,303	11,279	10,875	10,778	10,402
Government	12,431	12,855	13,281	13,653	13,331	13,048

The mining industry has always been cyclical, and lifelong residents of the region ("Rangers," as they proudly call themselves) are used to the occasional bad times. All miners are members of the United Steelworkers of America, and in addition to the relatively high wages they have been able to negotiate (starting wages range from roughly $10 per hour for laborers to $18 for electricians), those with 20 or more years of seniority receive supplemental unemployment benefits paid by the companies during layoffs. When working, these senior workers make well in excess of $20 per hour in wages and benefits, and often work overtime. The high wages, the supplemental benefits and the history of booms and busts have all contributed to a reduction in the mobility of much of the labor force in the region. More recently, Trade Adjustment Assistance has also been available.

It would seem that now the problems faced by the mines are more structural than cyclical. The eight taconite mines in the area are all subsidiaries of American steel companies, and therefore subject to the health, or relative lack thereof, of the domestic steel industry. Compounding that problem is the gradual reduction in the quality of the ore. It currently takes 22 tons of taconite ore to produce a ton of 85 percent pure iron pellets. The reduction in ore quality combined with the high costs of extraction make other worldwide sources, such as those in Brazil, strong competitors for what markets are available.

Unionized wages in the mines have affected wage levels in other industries and this, in addition to high transportation and energy costs, places the region at a disadvantage in attracting new firms. The region is rich in water and timber, but at present the timber industry remains rather undeveloped compared to similar areas in the northeastern and northwestern parts of the country. The wood products industry is also cyclical. A paper company in Grand Rapids recently postponed plans for a significant expansion. In addition, the shutdown of another wood products firm laid off 650 workers. Tourism, which has been hurt in the last few years by the overall state of the economy both in and outside the region, can be expected to show continued growth. However, jobs in this industry are seasonal and low wage, and cannot be expected to replace the economic loss suffered from the reduction in mining and mining-related employment.

The overall picture in the area is bleak. Unemployment is often concentrated in specific mining communities following major layoffs, and the repercussions on local economies have been devasting. For example, Babbitt, a town of 3,000 population, had an unemployment rate in excess of 80 percent over much of the past winter, and still had a rate of 50 percent during the summer of 1984. Local residents of Babbitt reported that there is concern that the local grocery will soon close, in large part because many people on food stamps drive 15 miles to

Ely to shop to avoid being seen using them. There have been similar closings of clothing stores, lumber yards, etc., in other communities throughout the Range. In most communities, there are substantial numbers of homes up for sale at what, to an outsider, look like bargain-basement prices.

Recently, there has been another round of shutdowns and layoffs. Table 4-3 indicates the current status of the eight mines in the region. At the end of this round of layoffs, total employment in the mines will have declined to roughly 3,200 from a peak of roughly 14,000 in 1981.

Currently, none of the companies is willing to predict a reopening or rehiring date, though all will say that it will not be until early 1985 at best. Production from the mines has been less than 50 percent of capacity for several years so that recent layoffs are affecting workers with 20 or more years of seniority. Many of those still working are on reduced work weeks. Reopenings will depend upon new contracts for taconite. However, these will have to be negotiated at a time when Brazilian ore is arriving in Cleveland at $12 to $15 less than the normal $52 per ton price for Iron Range pellets.

As the difficult times in the region continue, hope seems to be fading among many that there will soon be any significant recovery. People who had planned to leave only as a last resort are starting to pack. The outmigration that has occurred has been confined primarily to "non-Rangers," or outsiders attracted to the area by the wages in the mines. They are likely to have less seniority, so they have less chance of being recalled. They also have had less experience with the periodic bad times the region has endured in the past, are less attached to the area and, therefore, more willing to relocate. For some of the "Rangers," particularly the older ones with homes that are paid for and who can look forward to a vested retirement, leaving isn't even considered an option. These people "make out." Many have entered the tourism industry in varying ways as guides, outfitters, etc.; wood cutting is a common activity for many as well. It is not uncommon to see a yard almost filled with cut firewood to be sold or used to reduce fuel costs. Hunt-

Table 4-3
Status of Iron Range Taconite Companies

Company	Location	Employees at peak production in previous years*	Operating status	Approximate number of layoffs in latest round of shutdowns
Minorca	Virginia	510	Closed November 10	300
Butler Taconite	Nashwauk	600	Closed November 10	350
National Steel Pellet Co.	Keewath	1,000	Operating with about 600	—
Hibbing Taconite Co.	Hibbing	1,200	Closed November 10	900
Eveleth Mines	Eveleth	1,450	Operating with about 900	—
Erie Mining Co.	Hoyt Lakes	2,400	Plans to close December 2	940
Reserve Mining	Silver Bay Plant; Babbitt Mine	2,850	Cut production in half September 20; 200 laid off, about 600 placed on 32-hour work weeks	200
Minntac	Mountain Iron	4,400	Closed for 7 weeks August 5; plans to close again Saturday	1,800

SOURCE: *Minneapolis Star* and *Tribune*, November 16, 1984.

*Some jobs were eliminated by long-term production cutbacks or economies introduced after taconite demand dropped dramatically in 1981.

ing and fishing have gone beyond being sporting activities to being a source of food, complemented by extensive gardening.

Those who seem to be in the worst position are the ones with more than 12 but less than 20 years of seniority. Having run out of unemployment insurance and Trade Adjustment Assistance, they still face poor prospects of being recalled to the mines. At the same time, many employers are reluctant to hire them knowing that if a recall ever did occur, the higher wages would draw most of them back to the mines. Trying to hang on under such circumstances in growing increasingly difficult.

State Organization of Title III

Formally, all decisions regarding program funding and administration of JTPA in the State of Minnesota are made by the Governor's Job Training Council. The council performs the bulk of its work through committees, including one strictly for the dislocated worker program. The Dislocated Worker Committee includes several public sector council members, along with representatives from business and labor. The committee relies heavily on the staff of the Governor's Job Training Office (GJTO). This quasi-independent unit within the state's Department of Economic Security oversees all JTPA programs on a day-to-day basis. The executive director of GJTO reports directly to the commissioner of Economic Security and to the State Council, both of which have direct access to the governor. For Title III, the GJTO staff member for the Dislocated Worker Committee prepares all of the materials for the committee, helps with committee presentations before the State Council, and is the contact person for SDAs and other grant recipients.

Presently, the state Title III program does not appear to have a single focus. Reference is made to economic development and cases in which Title III funds are combined with other money, but most of the money is used to respond to particular groups of dislocated workers. An RFP process is now used to allocate virtually all of the state's Title III money.

The state has not established any eligibility requirements for the Title III program other than those defined in Section 302 of the federal legislation. There are no particular targeting requirements, although targeting occurs through the selection of proposals. The most heavily weighted criteria used in selecting proposals is the establishment of need. Typically, the screening committee has required that a survey of potential eligibles to identify needs and the services required be an integral part of these proposals. Thus, in a project like the Iron Range, there is relatively little targeting, even though a majority of the participants might have previously worked in the taconite mines.

The evaluation criteria used in selecting project proposals, and their respective weights, were as follows.

(1) Severity of need as described in the proposal. Unemployment rates and other measures, if any, that describe the severity of local economic conditions. Is it a one-industry area? How will the project affect the local need? (30 percent)

(2) The creativity, practicality, and probable effectiveness of the project as evidenced by the plan to implement the required components. (20 percent)

(3) Cost per participant. (20 percent)

(4) Plans for coordination with appropriate agencies, local elected officials, PICs or private employers, labor organizations and linkages with other employment-related programs. Utilization of a community task force with appropriate representation. (20 percent)

(5) Adequacy of fiscal and program management capabilities to administer the proposed program based on the Fiscal Administrative Capabilities Check List (a six-page list encompassing records, procedures, disbursements, audits, personnel policies, etc.). (10 percent)

Through the RFP process, the Iron Range Project has received roughly 35 percent of the state's Title III money, whereas by population, they would have received only 10 to 11 percent. Such disparity reflects the severity of the economic conditions in the region compared to the rest of the state.

Project Funding

During the transition year, the Iron Range Project received Title III money from four different sources: a project grant of $90,150 from the governor's 4 percent money under CETA; $250,000 from the state's FY83 and Emergency Jobs Bill (EJB) allocations (the Duluth SDA also received $250,000); $700,000 from the state's transition year (TY) allocation through the RFP process; and $600,000 from the Secretary of Labor's 25 percent discretionary fund.

The money from the governor's 4 percent grant was for a pilot project, consisting only of on-the-job and classroom training. From the FY83 and EJB allocations, the state designated both the Iron Range and Duluth for special allotments of $250,000 before dividing the rest of the money among the other eight prime sponsors in the state. These special allocations were based on the severity of structural unemployment in the Iron Range and Duluth relative to the rest of the state. Original plans for TY money called for holding 25 percent at the state level to allow for response to unanticipated plant closings, layoffs, etc. However, these plans were based on a predicted state allocation of $2.4 million. When only $1.018 million was received, all funds were distributed through the RFP process. The RFPs are now being staggered throughout the year to retain at least limited flexibility in responding to unforeseen problems.

The state has identified priorities for services, with job clubs/job search assistance, resume writing, skills assessment, etc., receiving top priority. This is followed by on-the-job and customized training; long-term classroom training and relocation is used as a last resort. For the Iron Range, it is pretty well accepted that the last resort has been reached, so that there is a heavy emphasis on long-term classroom training. Relocation is also an important part of the Iron Range service mix, although it is not actively promoted for political reasons. There have been no pressures from the state to alter the mix of services.

Service requirements are not imposed by the governor's special services plan. The plan identified performance goals for the transition year of 60 percent placement and cost per placement between $700 and $3,500, depending on the mix of services provided. No performance standards were adopted for Title III.

Indirectly, the state has discouraged the use of OJT in the service mix, though that influence comes from outside the JTPA system. Minnesota has had its own state jobs program (Minnesota Emergency Employment Development, or MEED) since May of 1983. The $70 million program does not have a training component, but allows employers to receive a subsidy of up to $4.00 per hour plus $1.00 for fringe benefits for a six-month period. With JTPA-OJT slots requiring a training component and reimbursing employers just 50 percent (or less) of wages for their training costs, many employers have found MEED slots more attractive, and as a result, OJT has been used less under JTPA in Minnesota than in many other states. With MEED tentatively scheduled to run out of funds in early 1985, OJT will receive more emphasis under JTPA during the 1984 program year.

Performance is monitored by the state and is compared to the goals identified in project proposals in evaluating refunding of projects, or new projects proposed by the same organizations. While those goals do not typically end up in contracts,the recipients are aware that they are expected either to come close to meeting them or to have a good explanation of why they could not.

The Nature of the Project

The grant recipient and administrative entity for all JTPA programs in the region is the Northeast Minnesota Office of Job Training (SDA3). They were also the prime sponsor under CETA. Some programs are operated by the SDA, while others are run jointly or subcontracted out. The major subcontractors are the Arrowhead Economic Opportunity Agency (Arrowhead), regional offices of the Minnesota Department of Economic Security, regional vocational schools and the Arrowhead Community College System, which is composed of five community colleges. Other contractors are used for specific, generally short-term training, such as Control Data, in Duluth, for data processing, several private truck driving schools, a welding course at Reserve Mining, and so on.

Arrowhead operates 40 percent of the region's OJT program (in addition to administering the MEED program for the region), Adult Basic Education Programs, and job club activities. Since 1965, Arrowhead has been the major social service agency in the region (as well as a CETA subcontractor). In addition to JTPA funding, Arrowhead receives funding from CSA, CDBG Social Services, Title XX, Weatherization, Older Americans Act, Housing Assistance, and other federal and state sources. Recently, Arrowhead received a special Title III grant, from discretionary money, in coordination with Hennepin County to assist in relocating 100 local residents to the Twin Cities area. Arrowhead is also a major Title IIA subcontractor in the region.

The Department of Economic Security operates 60 percent of the region's OJT program, and does job development, counseling, and intake. Satellite offices were set up in Silver Bay and Babbitt to make job search assistance more accessible to those in the outlying areas. Those offices, funded with Title III dollars, closed on September 30, 1984.

With the emphasis on longer term retraining, the community colleges and vocational schools have been heavily utilized. During the transition year, over 1,000 participants were involved in classroom training in 52 different schools throughout the state, the majority being community colleges and area vocational technical institutions (Vo-Tech), accounting for over 38 percent of program expenditures. Before funding programs at the schools, placement rates for the schools over the past two years are checked, and programs with placement rates of less than 50 percent are not funded.

Many of the Title III participants need upgrading and/or certification of skills. For example, truck drivers who have worked only in the mines often need an over-the-road certification that requires a two-week course. Welders in the mines are often trained in acetylene welding, but not in heliarc. To meet such needs, a variety of programs has been set up involving a variety of people, from employers to unions to Vo-Tech instructors.

SDA3 has coordinated with Trade Adjustment Assistance (TAA), but there have been some problems in doing so. The general pattern was for JTPA funding of tuition, and TAA funding mileage, allowances, etc. However, due to poor communications with the regional office, the regional TAA program has gone $250,000 in debt. SDA3 has 190 people originally funded under TAA halfway through training programs and no money available to allow them to complete the programs. The SDA is also strapped, because it did not receive a renewal of its discretionary grant and must therefore use its state funding to allow those enrolled under the TAA funds to complete their training before new participants can be enrolled.

An informal group has been set up to encourage coordination and avoid duplication of services in dealing with the problems of the region. The group has 17 members, including the SDA director, the regional Job Service director, the Arrowhead director, representatives from the community colleges and the Vo-Tech schools, the welfare agencies, local unions (primarily the steelworkers), and local chambers of commerce. To avoid competing with each other, they have agreed that the SDA should be the bidder on all RFPs, and they work with the PIC in selecting agencies, activities, funding levels, and so on. Unlike many other areas, state officials report that the coordination/partnerships are extremely good in SDA3. This supposition was supported during all conversations with those involved.

While not limited to miners, those unemployed from the mines are clearly the major target group for the project. Given their large numbers and the likelihood that unemployment for most will be long term, it is impossible to serve all of those who have lost jobs in the mines in the past three years. This raises a difficult question for program administrators. If there are insufficient funds to meet all the needs, should administrators focus on low-cost activities that maximize the number of people who can be served, or on higher cost long-term activities that will provide greater assistance to those who are served? In general, the latter strategy has been chosen. While low- cost activities like job search assistance are available, there are few jobs in the area that will satisfy miners who are used to much higher wages. As a result, most job search efforts are concentrated outside the area and, if successful, require relocation assistance, which raises the cost per participant. While many "non-Rangers" select the job search-relocation strategy, many natives choose longer term training. In some cases, this may still be very cost efficient, as many merely need skill upgrading or certification. For others, it often means a two-year classroom training program at community college or vocational school to learn new skills. No particular skill areas/industries are being targeted for postprogram placements. Before funding a classroom project at a vocational school, the SDA requires that it have a placement rate of 50 percent or greater for graduates over the past two years. This limits the selection of training areas available, but does not force people into areas in which they have no interest. Enrollments have been fairly high in electronics, computers and data processing, and skilled trades.

Initially, the state took the lead in helping the SDAs develop proposals for Title III funding. As the local partnerships began to develop, the state began to ease itself out and to merely provide notification of funding availability and technical assistance. The entire state is well aware of the severe problems faced in the northeast region. In addition, the governor is a Hibbing native, so there is no lack of sensitivity within the State Council or the Governor's Job Training Office to the problems in SDA3. This has not meant a rubber stamp approval for anything the region submits. The Dislocated Worker Committee will often send back proposals for further documentation of needs, such as a survey of the eligible population, or greater detail on how the proposed programs will be able to meet the identified needs. For this project, SDA3 conducted a survey of over 1,200 unemployed miners to identify their needs and what services would be necessary to meet their needs. As a consequence, the project was given the highest priority by the state because the needs were substantial and well established, and there was a comprehensive, well-designed plan to meet them.

From a programmatic point of view, there have been few changes from what was originally intended. The major change beginning to occur now is a somewhat greater emphasis on OJT in the service mix as the state's MEED dollars start to run out, though OJT will still not be the major component of the service mix. The real changes have been in the participants' attitudes; they are growing increasingly aware of the structural nature of their problems and are, in essence, being forced into unavoidable decisions. This realization has led to an increase in the use of relocation as an ultimate service, with some increase in remedial education, skills assessment, and counseling.

A number of private firms have been involved in retraining programs. A favorite of the SDA staff was a welding program in which Reserve Mining supplied the space, the electricity, electricians to convert 440 volt wiring to 220, and the stainless steel to be welded. The local union took care of printing and mailing flyers to those eligible for the program, and all the SDA had to do was schedule the training and pay the instructor. Similarly, Control Data was contracted to provide data processing training. Customized training has not been used extensively in the region, although when opportunities arise, it is used.

Basically, the unions have taken a realistic attitude toward the problems they are facing. A president of a union local indicated that they realize that many of their members are unlikely to ever be recalled to their old jobs, and given the limited opportunities currently available in the region, it is probably in the best interests of many of these people to move. The union's position is to help their members even though that obviously means smaller union roles in the future. Union representatives are members of the PIC and the informal program development group.

The unions have been actively involved in several programs, sometimes acting as the communications link between the programs and their members who are eligible, as in the welding program noted above. At other times, they provide the training, as they did in a two-week course to certify pipefitters.

The Eligible Population

Although a majority of the enrollees in the project have come from the mines, there are no particular eligibility requirements for enrollment beyond those established in the legislation. Most nonminers have probably become unemployed due to the problems in the mines, so there seems to be a justification for serving the general population, although nonminers may be more apt to be served under programs funded with state Title III dollars than with discretionary money.

Since a majority of participants come from the mines, they tend to be union members, to have higher than average prior wages, to have more years of work experience, and reasonably high levels of skill (although the skills may be largely industry-specific). Although education levels are fairly high, many have a need for adult basic education because they went directly from school to the mines and their basic skills have deteriorated over time.

Table 4-4 reports the characteristics of Title III program terminees during the transition year.

Program Services

There is no single service sequence for participants in this project; people go into different activities based on their needs, desires, and abilities. There are likewise no particular requirements for any program activities, although some screening takes place. Many participants go through vocational evaluation and assessment before selecting programs they will enter, and they are discouraged from entering an area in which they lack aptitude.

The numbers of participants by program activity during the transition year are shown below.

	Numbers of participants	Percent*
Classroom Training	304	23
Job Search	332	25
Relocation	122	9
OJT	74	6
Adult Basic Education	143	11
Vocational Evaluation & Assessment	101	8
Job Club	307	23
Total Participants	1,324	

*Percentages sum to more than 100 due to multiple services.

Table 4-4
Enrollment and Participant Characteristics During the
Transition Year, Selected Characteristics
October 1983 through June 1984

Selected characteristics	Number	Percent
Total participants	1,324	
Total terminations	801	
Entered employment	498	62
Other positive terminations	—	—
Other terminations	303	38
Sex		
Male	733	92
Female	68	8
Age		
14–15	—	—
16–19	—	—
20–21	53	7
22–44	646	81
45–54	77	10
55 and over	25	3
Education		
School dropout	78	10
High school graduate or more	723	80
Race		
White	792	99
Black	—	—
Hispanic	1	*
Native American	7	1
Asian	1	*
Employment barriers		
Limited English	2	*
Handicapped	7	1
Veteran	245	31
Substance abuse	3	*
Displaced homemaker	84	10
Benefit recipiency		
U.I. claimant	60	7

*Less than .5 percent.

Classroom training encompasses a wide variety of courses for participants. The majority are one-year and two-year programs, although many shorter term training classes have been developed for specific groups, as has been described previously. A listing of approved classroom training programs follows on table 4-5.

Table 4-5
Vocational/Occupational Programs
Arrowhead Community College Region

Approved One-Year Vocational Certificate Programs
    Accounting Technician
    Clerical
    Forestry Technician
    Practical Nursing
    Secretarial
    Small Engine Mechanic
    Welding

Approved Associate in Applied Science Programs
    Accounting Technician
    Clerical
    Drafting and Design Technology
    Environmental Analysis Technician
    Field Naturalist
    Human Services
    Law Enforcement
    Marketing
    Medical Secretary
    Natural Resources Technician
    Real Estate (Continuing Education)
    Nursing, A.D.
    Parks and Recreation Technician
    Physical Therapy Assistant
    Secretarial
      Option: Legal, Medical
    Water and Wastewater Technician

Approved Joint Occupational Programs

Program	Degree	Institutions
Medical Laboratory Technician	Associate in Applied Science	Hibbing Campus/ Hibbing AVTI
Law Enforcement	Associate in Applied Science	Arrowhead Colleges Hibbing AVTI

Certificate of Attendance

Program	Campus
Nurses Aides Geriatric	Itasca

Job clubs have been increased under JTPA relative to CETA. Operated by Arrowhead, there are currently clubs in 11 communities, operated by nine counselors. The structure seems to vary by area, with some being far more formal and structured than others. In the formal programs, the average duration is about two weeks, while it is generally a month in the others. In every case, there is a strong attempt to create a true club atmosphere so that there is a social environment with strong group support. The clubs provide job leads, as well as training in finding additional job leads, typing service, telephone, photocopying, newspapers containing help-wanted ads, assistance in preparing a job resume, training in interview skills, and a place where job seekers can concentrate on obtaining employment without distractions.

Job search assistance includes a number of the same activities as job clubs, including providing telephones (WATS lines, both in-state and out-of-state), newspapers, Employment Service Job Bank microfiche, and other sources of job openings, assistance with resume writing, and so on. A major part of job search assistance, however, is financial assistance for those unable to pay the costs of searching for employment. Given the experience and skills of most participants, many are employable immediately. However, having been unemployed for a long time, many have exhausted their resources, gone into debt and cannot afford, for example, to drive to Minneapolis for a job interview. In these cases, the SDA will pay for the transportation, meals, and lodging as necessary, with the only requirements being that interviews be set up in advance, be for an occupation the person is interested in, and can be documented. They have not had any problems with abuse of the program; the only person to miss a scheduled interview on a subsidized trip missed because of car trouble.

Vocational evaluation and assistance is also provided by Arrowhead. They have a fairly structured program, but it can be tailored to suit individual needs. The standard format is to undergo a two-day evaluation consisting of a battery of tests and hands-on experiences to determine aptitudes, academic achievement, vocational interests, vocational skills and abilities, intellectual functioning, work habits, and dexterity. Results are then evaluated jointly by a counselor and the participant in developing a vocational plan. Vocational research then identifies what programs are available to meet the individual's needs/desires, including examination of such things as financial aid programs and admission requirements for colleges. Most people are in the system for two to three weeks.

Adult Basic Education (ABE), again operated by Arrowhead, is an important program activity for many participants. There is a fairly high number of people who left school to work in the mines, or have simply not used their educational skills for so long that they have deteriorated. ABE is a program of services or instruction in which social skills are developed and ideas and experiences are shared, and in which basic academic and coping skills are developed. Clients determine their own learning goals, while instructors focus on learning needs rather than curricular standards. More formal programs, such as preparation for GED tests and ESL, are also provided.

Relocation is a part of the program that is not very popular among the staff. It is not promoted as an activity, though it is available to anyone who asks for it once they have secured employment in the new location. Thus far, most who have taken advantage of this activity are "non-Rangers." In addition to not wanting to force people to leave their homes, there is concern about the long-term effectiveness of relocation. While the regional economy will not be able to absorb all of the unemployed any time soon, and even if it could, it would be at drastically reduced wages, relocation often presents problems of its own. There have been several cases of someone relocating only to find that the new job was also terminated after six months. Families who try the Twin Cities area find that rents are considerably higher, as are other costs of living such as food, transportation, and child care, while wages are much lower, so that both parents are forced to work. Adaptation to the city is also difficult for people who come from an area where no one locks their doors, people on the street are friendly, and you needn't fear walking alone at night in any part of town. For many, however, there is no other choice, and relocation has been funded to all parts of the country, with the most frequent being the Twin Cities area, Alaska, and North Dakota.

The major counseling effort is job search skills training for participants who have substantial work experience but have not been in the job market in recent years. The layoffs in the mines have now gone deep enough to affect many with 20 or more years of seniority; consequently, many people have not been in the job market for a long time. Again, those with more than 20 years receive supplemental benefits from the companies, so they are not apt to be looking, but those between 10 and 20 years face dim prospects for being recalled. Most of this counseling takes place in the job clubs, with some in the less formal job search assistance program operated out of the ES offices.

Considerably less was said about counseling concerning wage expectations or personal problems, although both are occurring. Counseling with regard to wage expectations is probably the more prevalent, as few jobs in the area will offer wages anywhere near what people were getting in the mines, and wages for those relocating, while often higher than those available locally, are still likely to be significantly below the prior wages. Again, most of both types of counseling take place in the job clubs, with some of the coping problems dealt with in adult basic education programs.

Some selection takes place. When particular programs are set up, eligibles most suitable are channeled into them rather than taking whoever walks in the door. Between Title IIA and Title III, there are similarities as well as differences. For example, both titles have an electronics program providing classroom training. For the Title III program, however, enrollees must have some background in electronics. In general, Title III enrollees are much more likely to receive upgrading of skills and/or certification. A high percentage of those enrolled in classroom training programs extending over one or two years are Title III enrollees. The real problem currently faced is that many people were enrolled in long-term training activities last year using Trade Adjustment Assistance. When that money ran out this year and the discretionary grant was not refunded, it effectively froze enrollments so that last year's enrollees would be able to complete their training with state Title III funds. Letters were sent to some 500 people who were waiting for the new funding cycle but who will now be unable to enroll. As a result, frustration levels of both staff and participants were very high.

Individual job search with assistance provided is the primary service, but the philosophy here is that "anything goes." The exception is the limited number of OJT slots, where slots will not be funded without promise of continuation of employment after the training subsidy ends. This is again in contrast with the MEED program, where employers must pay the state back 70 percent of the subsidy received if they do not retain a person after the six-month subsidy period, but the percentage is gradually reduced to zero by 18 months after the subsidy. Relocation is funded only for those who have secured employment in their new location, so placement rates in that category are, by definition, 100 percent. They are usually the result of individual job search, perhaps aided through job search assistance.

Program Outcomes

With a placement rate of 62 percent during the transition year, one would have to say that the program is effective. However, both Arrowhead and the SDA staff indicate that roughly half of those placements have been outside the area (not all those relocating required relocation assistance, so the numbers on *table 4-6* do not reflect this). Again, given the severe conditions on the Range, there are simply not many jobs to be found in the region.

Outcome information is as follows: an average wage at entry of $18.00; an average wage at termination of $9.13; a cost per placement of $863.00; and a 62 percent placement rate for terminees.[1]

Costs per placement may go up as more of those who have gone through long-term training (OJT and classroom) begin to terminate, as shown in table 4-6. Entered employment figures are based on the last program activity before terminating, and so many understate rates for some activities, particularly assessment and basic education.

Table 4-6
Transition Year Termination and Placement Rate
by Program Activity

Transition year program activity	Participants	Terminations	Entered employment	
			Total	Rate
Job Search	332	317	162	51
Classroom	304	193	87	45
Relocation	122	122	122	100
OJT	74	6	4	67
Job Club	307	103	95	92
Adult Basic Education	143	33	23	70
Vocational Evaluation/Assessment	101	82	2	2
Job Development	3	3	3	100

Overall Assessment

In view of the conditions in this region, the project seems appropriate to the problem. There is a question of whether forms of lower cost training should be sought, such as more job club/job search activities, in order to serve more people, but such a strategy would probably be counterproductive. By emphasizing longer term types of training, in combination with job search assistance and relocation, they have been able to get reasonably high placement rates at wages that are around 50 percent of their prior level. And, at present, their costs per placement are low—under $900 per participant for the transition year with over 500 participants yet to terminate.

One problem seems to be with the timing of the funding *versus* the nature of the project. The project was started with discretionary funding, but a major service component was long-term community college course programs of up to two years. Despite the fact that they had documented the needs of the miners as required by the State Council Dislocated Worker Committee, and despite having a cost per participant of less than $1,000, the project was not refunded under the discretionary program, because, as one state official pointed out "Their costs were too high and their needs were not clearly identified." If discretionary projects are not to be refunded, then program planning should be limited to the period of funding. The effect has been to shut down the project while state funding pays for the balance of the program services committed earlier.

A final point is the use of very short-term programs to "certify" existing skills held by experienced, but dislocated workers. This is a low cost but effective program option that is particular to the Title III dislocated worker population.

NOTE

1. These figures were not readily available. A Random sample of 27 enrollees who had terminated from Job Search and Relocation yielded an average wage at placement of $9.13, which the staff felt might be a little low. They guessed that for most participants, the placement wage was about 50 percent of their wage including benefits prior to enrollment.

5
The Missouri Dislocated Worker Program
Job Search Assistance, Inc.

Introduction

The State of Missouri operates a statewide Dislocated Worker Program through three subcontractors. Two of them provide Title III services in Kansas City and St. Louis, the two major metropolitan areas of the state. Job Search Assistance, Inc. (JSA), a nonprofit organization, operates the Title III program in the nonmetropolitan areas under a performance-based contract with the state. JSA sets up offices in areas of the state experiencing problems with layoffs and plant closings. It was planned that job search assistance and OJT would be provided to 1,000 participants during the transition year by JSA.

The Origin of the Project

The Division of Manpower Planning (DMP) in the Department of Social Services administers all JTPA activities in Missouri. The director of DMP reports to the governor through the head of the Department of Social Services. DMP oversees the state's 15 SDAs through five field representatives. Since the Title III monies and the set-asides are all being operated as statewide programs, these activities are supervised by a statewide program coordinator.

Missouri's decision concerning the provision of Title III was based on two sources of information. First, DMP's Planning and Research Group produced a study entitled *Declining Industries and Dislocated*

71

Worker Job Training. Although this study was not formally published until August 1984, an earlier draft using data from 1982 was used in planning decisions for the areas to be served by the program.

The study identified 14 declining industries in Missouri, based on employment data over a 10-year period. Long-term unemployed workers from these industries were defined as those claiming unemployment insurance benefits for longer than the 14-week average period for the state. The report defines dislocated workers as long-term unemployed workers who have been displaced from declining industries. It concluded that, in 1983, there were 17,918 dislocated workers. When compared to the long-term unemployed, dislocated workers were slightly older and less concentrated in metropolitan areas. Their most recent employment was concentrated in manufacturing and mining. There were also certain occupational concentrations in the dislocated worker population.

The report also concluded that:

> The Missouri job training community has begun to recognize the unique reemployment problems of long-term unemployed workers displaced from declining industries. These individuals have little chance of returning to their previous industries and should be recruited for the JTPA dislocated worker program. Furthermore, since these declining industries are expected to continue losing employment, program participants should not be trained for such jobs unless this training is part of a comprehensive plan to induce long-term employment growth in currently declining industries or is locally necessary as an interim measure while economic growth and diversification strategies are undertaken.

DMP supplemented the report with special data runs which generated the dislocated worker totals for counties and SDAs. This information was combined with a second information source which might be called a visible indication of the need for Title III services: the Division of Employment Security's plant shutdowns and layoff report.

State Organization of Title III

On the basis of this research, the decision was made to operate the Title III as a statewide program targeting roughly one-third of the funds to each of the two major metropolitan areas (St. Louis and Kansas City), with the remaining one-third allocated to outstate areas. No funds were formula-funded to any SDA.

The goals for Title III project funding were twofold. First, funding was provided for several large OJT projects, mainly with automobile manufacturers. Second, projects covering each of the three targeted geographic areas were funded. These projects emphasize job search assistance efforts.

Given the economic conditions at that time, DMP believed that focusing Title III projects on job search assistance provided the best and least costly means of putting Missouri's experienced dislocated workers back to work. The approach is consistent with meeting the needs of specific target populations while complementing Missouri's overall emphasis on maximizing the economic development impact of JTPA. In addition to the use of some Title III monies for OJT, the 8 percent set-aside money under Title IIA was reserved entirely for customized training. SDAs were required to set aside an additional 10 percent of their funds for this purpose.

DMP decided to retain control over Title III funding. They felt that operating the Dislocated Worker Program as a statewide program would provide greater assurance that funds could be utilized during the transition year. This allowed the new PICs to become operational without also having to work with Title III programming. In addition, DMP could target Title III activities to areas with greater need, based on the Division's research on the location of displaced workers.

Once the statewide program decision was made, DMP turned to established program operators in each of the three targeted geographical areas of the state to run the programs. Job Search Associates, Inc., was selected to operate the program in all other areas outside the St. Louis and Kansas City metropolitan areas. This three-way division of the state corresponded to the distribution of displaced workers, approximately one-third of whom were estimated to be in each of the three areas.

DMP reviews a monthly report from the Missouri Division of Employment Security, entitled "Significant Layoffs and Census by SDA Area." DMP's knowledge of plant closures and layoffs together with the dislocated worker study led to the selection of six cities in which JSA was to open offices during the transition year. The cities were Joplin, Neosho, Mexico, St. Joseph, Springfield and Flat River. The six cities are located in five SDAs. For program year 1984, DMP identified three additional cities in which offices were opened—Independence, Hannibal, and Jefferson City.

The eligibility criteria for the statewide Title III program were those specified in the JTPA legislation. However, DMP made it clear that it expected the operators to concentrate on the first two definitions found in the Act. Providing services to long-term unemployed who were eligible for Title IIA programs was definitely not a goal in Missouri. Instead, the focus by DMP was on dislocated workers identified through their research.

DMP's service strategy emphasizes job search assistance. On-the-job training services were included to provide a comprehensive program for the Title III participants. Missouri officials believed that dislocated workers eligible for Title III would benefit most from returning to work as quickly as possible. The workers already had motivation, job-related skills and training, and good work records, but needed assistance in locating job opportunities. It was felt that relatively few dislocated workers would desire classroom training. Job search assistance was the key service element so that dislocated workers with substantial experience, but who had not sought a job for some time, could acquire the job search skills that would result in their early employment. It was recognized that some workers would need the additional assistance of OJT.

DMP's view of the appropriate service mix was reinforced by a task force established to suggest strategies for Title III programming. Task force members reviewed existing dislocated workers programs, especially the Downriver project in Michigan, the Des Moines, Iowa Mayor's Task Force on Plant Closings and Job Retraining, and the Canadian Manpower Consultative Service. Staff members also attended the first National Conference on the Dislocated Worker. DMP memoranda on various aspects of Title III were written in March and April 1983.

Based on the review by the task force, DMP recommended a four-tiered approach to providing services for dislocated workers. The tiered approach was proposed to take into account different needs of dislocated workers in urban *versus* rural areas and differences in the workers' "attachment" to the labor force. The tiers are as follows:

(1) Statewide services – a statewide program aimed at dislocated workers collecting UI benefits. It was noted that . . . "this approach would expand to incorporate the rural areas of the State where there are pockets of dislocated workers (i.e., Washington County)";

(2) Community Based Programs in Urban Centers – funding for agencies with broad local support in St. Louis and Kansas City;

(3) Pre-Shutdown Plant Intervention – programs developed by the State Council of the AFL-CIO and the Human Resource Development Institute;

(4) Concentrated local political jurisdictions – using local PICs to provide services to workers facing layoff due to plant closings.

JSA provides statewide tier 1 services in all areas outside the St. Louis and Kansas City metropolitan areas.

DMP set performance standards for Title III operators based on historical experience under CETA. The entered employment performance standard was set at 60 percent for the transition year. The average wage was set at $4.29 per hour. Because DMP negotiated a unit-price contract with JSA, it was not necessary to include a performance standard for cost per placement. Instead, JSA received payments on the following schedule.

Hourly wage at placement	Payment amount per placement
Less than $3.60	No payment
$3.60 to $4.56	$1,341.88
$4.56 or above	$1,677.35

This contract is the only statewide performance-based contract in Missouri. The payment schedule was determined by negotiations between DMP and JSA, beginning with a line item budget. This negotiated budget was then converted to the unit-price contract.

During the program year, the payment schedule under JSA's unit-price contract has been expanded to provide three levels of payment dependent upon the hourly wage at placement.

Hourly wage at placement	Payment amount per placement
Less than $3.50	No payment
$3.50 to $4.24	$1,341.88
$4.25 to $4.71	$1.677.35
$4.72 or above	$1,845.09

The Local Labor Market

Since JSA operated offices in six cities in five DSAs during the transition year, the primary area served by each office will be discussed. Table 5-1 summarizes the local labor market for each area. The selected labor market information presented in the table is for March 1983 when initial Title III decisions were made. Data are reported for areas smaller than SDAs as an indication of the labor market conditions in the immediate area served by the JSA office. For offices opened during the transition year, the civilian labor force ranged from 10,898 in Audrain County (Mexico) to 111,707 in the Springfield SMSA. Unemployment rates ranged from 9.3 percent in Springfield to 14.6 percent in St. Francois County (Flat River). The overall unemployment rate in Missouri during the period was 11.6 percent. Although the larger SMSA units tend to have lower overall unemployment rates, they have had a number of plant closings.

Table 5-1
Selected Labor Market Information by Job Search Assistance, Inc., Office Location

Office	Data unit	Civilian labor force	Unemployment rate	Weekly earnings	Employment in selected industry groups (thousands)				
					Mfg.	Trade	Service	Govt.	Total
Transition year									
Joplin Neosho	Joplin SMSA	58,249	10.9	$277	14.1 (31.2)	10.6 (23.5)	8.0 (17.7)	6.1 (13.5)	45.2 (100.0)
St. Joseph	St. Joseph SMSA	46,666	13.2	286	8.3 (23.9)	8.7 (24.1)	7.6 (21.0)	6.1 (16.9)	36.1 (100.0)
Springfield	Springfield SMSA	111,707	9.3	284	17.4 (19.9)	24.0 (27.5)	21.2 (24.3)	12.3 (14.1)	87.4 (100.0)
Mexico	Audrain Co.	10,898	14.0	284	2.2 (27.2)	1.9 (23.5)	1.2 (14.8)	1.8 (22.2)	8.1 (100.0)
Flat River	St. Francois Co.	19,424	14.6	227	2.2 (19.6)	2.6 (23.2)	2.5 (22.3)	2.6 (23.2)	11.2 (100.0)
Program year									
Independence	Jackson Co.	76,805	9.2	343	60.3 (18.8)	75.4 (23.5)	75.1 (23.4)	51.3 (16.0)	320.7 (100.0)
Hannibal	Marion/Ralls LMA	18,207	14.8	238	2.1 (19.6)	2.2 (20.6)	2.7 (25.2)	2.0 (18.7)	10.7 (100.0)
Jefferson City	Cole/Osage LMA	35,922	8.9	257	2.6 (8.0)	6.7 (20.6)	5.5 (16.9)	13.3 (40.8)	32.6 (100.0)
	Missouri totals	2,341,842	11.6	427	390.9 (20.7)	447.2 (23.7)	404.7 (21.4)	331.8 (17.5)	1,889.6 (100.0)

Employment data by broad industry groups for the Joplin SMSA (Joplin and Neosho) indicate that the area has a higher concentration of manufacturing, 31 percent compared to 21 percent in Missouri as a whole. Services and government employment are proportionately lower. The area has had a number of plant closings resulting in a need for Title III services.

St. Joseph's industrial distribution of employment is similar to the overall Missouri averages. However, the area has been particularly hard hit by plant closings (including the loss of 300 jobs in 1983 due to the shut-down of a meat packing plant).

Springfield has slightly higher concentrations of employment in the trade and service sectors than the statewide averages. Government employment is somewhat less than average. The local economy illustrates a mixed trend that includes both growing and declining industries. Plant closings and layoffs have also been a factor in Springfield.

Mexico, in Audrain County, has experienced a number of significant plant closings. Most recently, the Aero Drapery Company closed, resulting in a loss of 160 jobs. Employment in the area is higher than average in the manufacturing and government sectors with services employing only 15 percent of the total compared to a Missouri average employment in services of 21 percent.

The Flat River office in St. Francois County also draws dislocated workers from Washington County where the unemployment rate in March 1983 was 29.8 percent, the highest in the state. The employment distribution pattern in St. Francois County is similar to that of the state.

DMP essentially required that JSA focus its attentions on dislocated workers according to the first two definitions under the act. At the same time, JSA does not turn down individuals who are otherwise eligible. In order to serve clients who are also Title IIA eligible, JSA must document that the client does not want to be referred to the SDA in the area. This procedure seems to work satisfactorily.

All eligibles are served, but outreach and recruitment efforts attempt to locate long-term dislocated workers. Generally, the wages previously received by dislocated workers appear to be above the average of the local labor market, particularly when dealing with experienced, skilled workers with long work histories at closed industrial plants.

The Nature of the Project

Job Search Assistance, Inc., provides Title III services in the targeted geographical areas. The service areas were selected by DMP for their statewide effort, excluding the St. Louis and Kansas City areas which are served by other operators. JSA established and operates an office in each of the target areas. DMP selected JSA as a provider of the statewide Title III services based on a long history of successful involvement in job search assistance programs.

The director and core staff of JSA became involved in job search assistance programs when they worked for DMP and operated an Employment Opportunities Pilot Program (EOPP) in Missouri. This program, one of 15 in the United States, was funded by the U.S. Department of Labor (DOL) and the Department of Health, Education and Welfare. The Missouri pilot program operated from October 1978 to March 1982 in eight counties which had been selected by DOL. The specific program was designed by the State of Missouri, but as part of the national demonstration it had to include job search activities as a major component. The program was for WIN registrants and provided eight weeks of job search assistance. If participants were not successful in obtaining unsubsidized positions during these eight weeks, they were placed in work training. During this time, the development of JSA's present manual was begun. The Missouri program proved successful enough that the director provided technical assistance to several other sites.

When the EOPP program was completed, DMP decided to use the staff to train Community Action Program (CAP) staff in selected CETA balance-of-state areas in conducting job search assistance programs. This effort was conducted between April and September 1982. The former

EOPP staff trained CAP staff in Springfield, Columbia, Joplin, St. Joseph, West Plains and Sedalia (previously an EOPP site). The operating procedures used in EOPP were further tested and refined. Participants in these job search assistance programs were volunteers (CETA Title IIB participants) with higher levels of motivation than had been noted in working with WIN mandatory registrants. Additionally, CAP programs operated in urban and rural areas, while EOPP had been located principally in rural areas. The programs placed a total of 800 participants during the six months.

During the final year of CETA, training was expanded to a total of 15 CAPs. CETA funding was augmented by Community Services Block Grant funds of $322,000. CAP programs had a combined goal of 900 jobs and actually placed 1,400. During this time, the manual underwent further refinement with reduction of time spent on directed job search activities from eight to four weeks. At this time, the key staff that later formed JSA had extensive experience in operating and conducting training for job search assistance activities. This experience had been gained with WIN and CETA participants, in urban and rural locations.

It was to utilize this expertise that DMP turned to JSA, which was incorporated as a not-for-profit corporation in July 1983 by the core staff that had begun in October 1978. Both DMP and JSA believe that job search activities are ideal for dislocated workers who have some skills and a high level of motivation as evidenced by their work histories. It was felt that JSA could be successful with dislocated workers since it had proven its effectiveness with welfare and CETA participants.

DMP selected the sites for Title III operations. DMP notified the PIC in a selected SDA that JSA would be opening an office to provide Title III services in that area. JSA begins by making an informational presentation on the program at a PIC meeting. It requires participants to be registered with the appropriate Employment Service (ES) office. The majority of linkages between JSA and employers are contacts made for recruiting and placement purposes. Since many of the areas have low levels of union membership, JSA's main contact with employers covered by collective bargaining agreements often occurs when setting up an on-the-job training contract with a company. In such cases, it obtains concurrence from the bargaining agent before proceeding with OJT operations.

All participants receive up to three weeks of job search assistance. If they have not located an unsubsidized position at the end of three weeks, efforts are made to place them in an OJT position. During the transition year, 576 out of 963 left the job search assistance component for an unsubsidized job after, on average, 6.5 sessions. An additional 100 were enrolled in OJT.

JSA can serve any individual who is eligible for Title III services. The long-term unemployed are served only if they have been actively seeking work, i.e., meet the labor force definition of "unemployed." Typically, JSA's offices draw most heavily from the geographic areas nearest the office. Any eligible applicant will be placed in the job search assistance component within five days of application with new classes beginning each Monday afternoon.

In addition to the virtual absence of a waiting period, the JSA program is notable for its performance-based contracts. Under this unit-price contract JSA only receives payments for placements at wages above $3.59 per hour. Employer reimbursements made for OJT contracts are deducted from JSA's payment, or, more accurately, are counted as an expense. JSA uses a voucher procedure and only reimburses the participating company if the individual is hired after the OJT contract period. This has the benefit of improving the commitment of employers to the individual under OJT. For example, companies are more willing to work with trainees and to have JSA provide additional counseling to help them move into an unsubsidized position.

JSA does not generally provide industry-specific Title III services. Due to the statewide nature of the program, it is difficult to generalize about the types of industries and former occupations represented by the participants. Since the economies of many rural areas are dominated by a single major employer, a layoff or plant closing disrupts the entire local economy. The broad industry group which most frequently triggers this is manufacturing. However, in the Jefferson City area, a number of workers lost construction-related jobs when Union Electric Company's Callaway nuclear plant was completed. The prime contractor, Daniels International, had used a number of workers from the counties in SDA 5 (JSA's Mexico and Jefferson City offices are in SDA 5). The state's report on declining industries identifies 14 at the two-digit SIC level. These include mining, food and kindred products, apparel, leather, and transportation equipment.

A major determinant in DMP's decision to utilize JSA for statewide services was their past record. A second important factor was the short response time that JSA could provide in setting up a local office operation. In a typical situation JSA enters a new area and begins operation in three to four weeks. In a hypothetical example, an area coordinator will go into an area and contact a realtor for space, place advertisements for personnel, and obtain phone service and furniture. A local office, with a weekly enrollment goal of 10, is staffed by an assessment counselor, job counselor, community relations representative (similar to a job developer), and a clerical worker. After resumes are screened, the director of operations assists in the hiring decision. Existing JSA staff are initially sent to assist new staff in outreach. New workers are enrolled in the first job club run by JSA to train the local staff. They then conduct the next two job clubs, and are critiqued by a representative of JSA. Because JSA has operated and trained for so long, the process goes relatively smoothly.

As the project has been implemented for dislocated workers, some changes have been made in the operations manual. The manual had been developed for use with welfare recipients and then CETA participants, and some changes were warranted for the Title III population. Generally, these changes added some sophistication to the presentations to take cognizance of the previous work experience and the expected higher motivation of dislocated workers.

For the program year, JSA has intensified its OJT efforts as a result of DMP's insistence. DMP's view is that job search assistance programs must include an OJT option to provide a comprehensive employment and training approach for dislocated workers. This increased OJT emphasis has been beneficial for participant recruiting since it puts JSA in contact with employers who are not laying off workers. JSA's position is that they can offer some service to any employer. If a company is hiring, it can screen and provide quality workers. Companies laying off can be a source of program participants for job search assistance services and this also helps the company from a public relations point of view. A company that is neither hiring nor laying off can provide JSA with referrals of company job applicants. This assists the company, since it can avoid taking job applications while also helping job seekers.

Local private sector representatives are not directly involved in the planning and implementation of the program. However, DMP's overall statewide strategy for Title III was approved by the Missouri Job Training Coordinating Council and the governor. Also, JSA has developed close contacts with many employers in each of its primary service areas.

Unions are not directly involved with the program, either. However, this can be largely attributed to the lower incidence of unions in rural Missouri as opposed to St. Louis and Kansas City. JSA obtains prior approval from collective bargaining agents for OJT contracts with covered employers.

Program Services

All participants receive the same service sequence. Potential applicants have an opportunity to attend a daily orientation. If interested, they are scheduled for a formal application and eligibility process. If eligible, they begin in the job club the following Monday afternoon. The job search assistance provided through the job club is the primary service, and continues for a maximum of three weeks. Attempts are then made to place any remaining participants in OJT positions. Details of all phases of program services follow.

Outreach and Recruitment

The JSA community relations representative makes a broad range of community contacts both with employers and sources of applicants. In some cases, he advertises job openings and uses job clubs as a mechanism to screen prospective employees for companies. Additional outreach techniques include newspaper advertisements, television and radio shows and public service announcements, JSA business cards or signs at employers, and occasionally, direct access to employer applicant files. Employers and newspaper ads have proven to be the most useful tools.

Orientation and Intake

Orientation and intake are conducted in four phases as an ongoing process. First, all prospective participants are asked to complete general applications separate from the official intake applications, and make an informal declaration of the Title III program they believe best represents their situation. Second, the program's goals and philosophy are explained at daily orientation sessions. Third, interested individuals are prescreened after the orientation sessions and provided with a list of documentation required for the formal intake interview which is then scheduled. Fourth, the formal intake interview is conducted by the assessment counselor. At this time, eligibility is determined and an Employability Development Plan is completed, all program forms and releases are signed (releases are obtained for previous work references, providing participant information, receiving information from hiring companies, and the complaint and grievance procedure), and the JTPA intake form is completed. Referrals to other programs are made if the JTPA intake form indicates referral to vocational rehabilitation or JTPA Title IIA. Applicants are also sent to Employment Service to register. All eligible applicants are scheduled to begin the job club the following Monday.

Job Club—Week One

Job search assistance activity uses a structured job club approach. The job club meets four hours each afternoon during the first week. Sessions are conducted by the job counselor. After the first day, each participant is expected to have two job interviews with employers each day. The main daily activities or topics are indicated below.

Day 1

- Presentation of job search work policies and the signing of the counselor/job seeker agreement;
- Successful interviewing;
- Interview questions;
- Leads;
- Obtaining three letters of recommendation; and
- Completion of sample application.

Day 2

- Resume preparation;
- Interview question responses;
- List of ten job leads;
- Phone outline introduction;
- Writing qualifying statements for use in phone contact; and
- Role-playing telephone outline.

Day 3

- Rehearse interview questions;
- Review telephone outline; and
- Present telephone rebuttals.

Day 4

- Follow-up calls and letters of recommendation; and
- Presentation of personal appearance and body language.

Day 5

- Continue phone contacts;
- Job-keeping skills; and
- Mock interviews.

Job Club—Weeks Two and Three

Participants who have not found unsubsidized employment continue job club activities in the morning of weeks two and three. These sessions provide additional follow-up and reinforcement to the job club's week one material. Activities in weeks two and three are somewhat less structured. However, participants are required to make five personal contacts daily. These must include at least three interviews with a company person who can hire and fire people.

On-the-Job Training

The job counselor and the community relations representative work in close contact concerning participants. Usually after the first week the counselor can determine whether or not a participant may need to gain entry to an employer using an OJT contract. The community relations representative is continuously contacting employers for direct placement opportunities and on-the-job training positions.

Due in part to JSA's unit-price contract which provides no JTPA reimbursement unless the hourly wage exceeds $3.60 and the fact that OJT payments to employers are expenses to JSA, OJT contracts are only written at wages above $3.60 per hour. Additionally, the employer's commitment to the trainee's success is strengthened because the job search voucher system only reimburses employers if the participant is hired in an unsubsidized position after the OJT period. Employers receive no payments for participants they terminate or who quit. This procedure reduces the exposure of JSA to incurring expenses not associated with placements, but, more importantly, it gives the employers a stake in achieving success with each OJT participant.

Employment Verification

JSA's unit-price contract with DMP requires that every placement be verified to establish the correct payment which is based on hourly wage at placement. All placements are verified, even those for which JSA receives no compensation (those below $3.60 per hour). JSA converts the verification process into a job/participant development contact by requiring that the community relations representatives take the verification form to employers in person. This gives the JSA representative an opportunity to begin contacts with new employers when participants have secured their own job, which is often the case.

Counseling plays an important ongoing role in JSA's program. The primary focus of the job club activity is to provide the experienced dislocated worker with the job search skills necessary to become re-employed. JSA data for the transition year indicate the average participant who obtains employment attends 6.5 sessions and goes to 6.6 interviews before obtaining a job. Note that these outcomes have been achieved in rural and smaller urban areas which have relatively high levels of unemployment.

Counseling is also utilized to overcome the two main attitudinal obstacles faced by dislocated workers: they were initially not expecting the layoff, and many expect to be called back to work by their previous employer. These two attitudes must be overcome in order to successfully proceed in the job club. As illustrated by the labor market information provided above, most of the areas where JSA operates have below average wages for the state. While the experienced dislocated worker may have received wages above the area average based on industry affiliation, skill level or tenure, many do not have to make as major an adjustment in wage expectations as do workers in large urban areas with higher pay scales and greater union representation. This reduces the need for extensive wage expectations counseling. However, it is still necessary to counsel participants that starting in a new job will probably mean beginning at a lower wage rate.

Program Participants

Table 5-2 presents enrollment and participant characteristics for the transition year and the first six months of program year 1984. Participants have been predominantly white males between the ages of 22 to 44. This pattern appears consistent with the typical dislocated worker one would expect in the areas where JSA offices are located.

Table 5-2
Enrollment and Participant Characteristics Period:
Transition Year and Program Year 1984 (6 months)

Selected characteristics	TY 1984	Percent	PY 1984	Percent
Total participants	963		2,030	
Total terminations				
Entered employment	735	76	1,186	58
Other positive terminations	576	60	1,017	50
Other terminations	159	17	169	8
Sex				
Male	601	62	1,179	58
Female	362	38	851	42
Age				
14-15	—	—	—	—
16-17	1	*	1	*
18-21	101	10	204	10
22-44	697	72	1,498	74
45-54	122	13	242	12
55 and over	42	4	85	4
Education				
School dropout	140	15	241	12
Student (H.S. or less)	—		—	
High school graduate	535	56	776	38
Past high school	288	30	1,013	50
Race				
White	922	96	1,925	95
Black	25	3	76	4
Hispanic	3	*	13	1
Native American	7	1	8	*
Asian	6	1	8	*
Employment barriers				
Limited English	6	1	5	*
Handicapped	13	1	34	2
Offender	24	2	54	2
Other	—		—	
Benefit recipiency				
U.I. claimant	302	31	820	40
U.I. exhaustee	152	16	203	10
Public assistance (GA)	7	1	13	1
AFDC	34	4	37	2
Youth AFDC	—		—	
Labor force status (prior 26 weeks)				
Unemployed 1-14 weeks	252	26	695	34
Unemployed 15 or more weeks	674	70	1,240	61

*Less than .5 percent.

Most participants have at least a high school diploma with almost 30 percent having completed schooling beyond high school. During the transition year, 47 percent of participants were receiving UI benefits or had exhausted the benefits. Approximately 70 percent had been unemployed 15 weeks or longer.

JSA can provide service to all eligible individuals. However, DMP has stipulated that they concentrate their efforts on persons meeting the first two definitions of a dislocated worker in the JTPA Act. All participants receive identical services.

Program Outcomes

JSA's job development/placement process places primary responsibility on the individual. The job search assistance activities undertaken during the job club sessions stress that most available jobs are in the hidden job market. These jobs can be found by using the tested approaches learned in the job club sessions. The JSA technique involves the use of telephone contacts to develop interview opportunities so that participants have a chance to demonstrate their skills and work experience record.

This approach is augmented by job development for direct placement which is conducted by the JSA community relations representative. More important, the representative develops on-the-job training positions for use by participants who have been unsuccessful in three weeks of job club.

During the transition year, all Title III contractors had performance standards written into their contracts. DMP expected an entered employment rate of 60 percent with an "other positive termination rate" of 5 percent. The average hourly wage standard was set at $4.29. JSA had no performance standard for cost per placement because it operated on a unit-price contract. For program year 1984, the entered employment performance standard was increased to 65 percent and the other positive termination rate remains unchanged at 5 percent. Selected performance indicators for both time periods follow.

	Transition year	Program year (6 mos.)
Average hourly wage at termination (of those placed)	$4.69/hour	$5.08/hour
Cost per placement	$1,023	$1,300 (est.)
Proportion of terminees placed	78%	86%
Wage replacement rate	83%	80%

It should be noted that the rising cost per placement is caused by the higher entered employment rate at increased wage levels achieved during the first six months of program year 1984. Since the terms of unit-price contract provides higher payments for higher wage rates, JSA has received higher payments in the first six months of the program year as a result of improved performance.

Overall Assessment

JSA's Title III operations have several important aspects which contribute to its success. First, key personnel have extensive experience operating job search assistance programs dating back to 1978. Second, their expertise has enabled them to revise their operations manual to take account of the changing environments in which they have operated. For example, JTPA Title III services are provided to dislocated workers, most of whom have good previous work records and higher skill levels than the welfare and CETA populations served previously. Third, past experience enables JSA to identify and hire quality staff for their local offices. Fourth, in addition to hiring quality staff, the company believes in keeping them motivated. Fifth, the company can draw on their experience to start up new offices and begin providing job clubs quickly (within approximately 30 days). Sixth, JSA's policy of providing employer reimbursement for OJT only if the participant is hired seems to improve the employer's commitment; it is also in JSA's interest, given their unit-price contract. Last, JSA's performance-based contract with DMP focuses attention on attaining unsubsidized placements at relatively high wage levels.

Based on the goals and objectives of DMP's statewide Title III effort emphasizing job search activities, the JSA program is achieving high employment rates at wages above the statewide average wage performance standard. Costs per placement are low compared to other program strategies.

The program appears to be appropriate for the eligible population. For example, during the first six months of program year 1984, the average participant who was placed attended 6.4 sessions and had 5.8 interviews before obtaining a job. The 86 percent employment rate and average wage of $4.94 are considerably above planned levels. JSA's goal for the entire program year is 1,250 placements. In the first six months, 1,017 participants found unsubsidized employment.

6
The Hillsborough, North Carolina Dislocated Worker Project

Introduction

The Dislocated Worker Program observed in this case study is located in the town of Hillsborough, in Orange County, North Carolina. The project was funded to provide Title III services for approximately 400 workers affected by the closure of the Cone-Mills textile plant. Program services offered by this project included job search instruction; direct job placement; and, to a lesser extent, on-the-job and classroom training. The project began operation in December 1983 and ended in March 1985.

The Local Labor Market

The Hillsborough Title III project is located in the Orange County labor market area. Labor market data for this county are reported on both a monthly and an annual basis. Annualized data for 1984, monthly employment figures for 1984, and annualized employment and wage data for 1983 are used to provide a description of the Orange County labor market. Table 6-1 provides the estimated number of persons employed in Orange County by industry for 1983.

In 1983, the Orange County labor market provided employment for 33,000 people. An important characteristic of this labor market is its diversity. Although the largest employer, the government, employs approximately 58 percent of the workforce, no other single industry provides a significant proportion of total employment. More important, the declining manufacturing sector employs slightly less than 10 percent of the Orange County workforce. The largest manufacturing industry in the county is textiles, but textiles employs less than 3 percent of the total workforce of Orange County.

Table 6-1
Labor Market Data for Orange County During 1983

Industry	Number of employees
Nonmanufacturing	
Government	19,350
Trade	5,750
Service	3,900
Construction	940
Manufacturing	
Textile	940
Printing	440
Lumber and wool	210
Other manufacturing*	1,470
	33,000**

SOURCE: Employment Security, Durham, North Carolina.
*This category includes the food, apparel, furniture, chemistry, rubber, stone glass cleaning, nonelectrical machinery, electrical machinery, and transportation industries.
**This figure does not include persons who work two jobs or commute in and out of the community, and agriculture workers.

A favorable result of this diversity has been that employment declines in one particular industry have not appreciably affected overall employment levels. Evidence is found in the Orange County unemployment rates. Monthly unemployment rates for the area during 1984 fluctuated from a low of 2.7 percent to a high of 5 percent. The average annual unemployment rate for 1984 was only 3.7 percent. The director of the Durham Employment Security office stated that the unemployment levels for Orange County have historically been the lowest in the state.

Table 6-2 shows the relative growth in employment by industry from December 1983 to December 1984.

Table 6-2
Relative Growth in Employment by Industry
in Orange County, North Carolina

Type of industry	Employment growth (percent)
Nonmanufacturing	5
Construction	16
Trade	6
Service	5
Government	2
Manufacturing	6
Electrical machines	20
Textile	-29
Apparel	-14

SOURCE: Employment Security, Durham, North Carolina.

Overall, employment in the county during 1984 grew by 5 percent in nonmanufacturing and 6 percent in manufacturing. However, behind this apparent stability are serious employment problems in the textile and apparel industries. While employment grew in manufacturing, the textile and apparel industries experienced declines of 29 and 14 percent, respectively.

The Origin of the Hillsborough Title III Project

The textile mill in Hillsborough began production of woven fabric in 1846. The plant was purchased by the Cone-Mills Corporation of Greensboro, North Carolina, in the early 1950s. During a span of 30 years, Cone-Mills became the largest firm in Hillsborough (a town of roughly 3,000 residents) and the second largest firm in Orange County. Offering relatively high wages and stable employment in a small town, Cone-Mills was a significant element in the tax base of the town and in the Hillsborough business district.

The problems of the textile industry in general, and the Cone-Mills company in particular, are longstanding. The textile industry has been faced with strong international competition that benefits from much lower labor costs and the use of modern technology. This competition has placed pressure on the textile industry to become less labor-intensive and more mechanized.

However, like other textile companies in the South, the Cone-Mills Corporation was particularly hard hit by the recessions of the 1970s and early 1980s. When the economic recovery began following the 1981 recession, the ability of Cone-Mills to invest in more modern equipment was weakened by foreign competition. As a consequence, the Cone-Mills Corporation announced plans to reduce its workforce by 1984.

A statewide survey of 58 major firms found similar problems among other textile companies. Twelve of the 15 firms reporting employment declines in 1984 were textile companies. During the same year, 61 textile plants closed in North and South Carolina as the industry reduced its workforce by 19,500.

A primary part of the Cone-Mills workforce reduction was the Hillsborough plant. When the plant closing was announced in December 1983, Cone-Mills employed 550 people. When the plant closed in spring 1984, a total of 416 employees received "pink slips." Management from the plant indicated that approximately 130 employees left Cone-Mills during the period after the closing date was announced and before the plant actually closed.

The economic effect of the closing was immediately felt in this small town. At the time of the observation for this case study, the small businesses which surrounded the plant were boarded shut. The town's historic district, which depends upon tourism, was still in operation. However, the small businesses in the historic section of Hillsborough offered few, if any, job opportunities for the laid-off Cone-Mills workers.

For several months, buoyed by rumors of a possible buy-out by another textile firm and supported by unemployment benefits, many former employees waited for possible reemployment at the plant. This optimism disappeared and the reality of their situation became obvious, however, when the Cone-Mills Corporation removed all useful equipment from the Hillsborough plant to its operation in Greensboro. Not long afterward, the plant was boarded shut. To the most optimistic observer, the plant was shut for good.

Organization of Title III in North Carolina

JTPA in North Carolina is organized in the Department of Natural Resources and Community Development. Within this cabinet level agency, responsibility for both Title IIA and Title III is lodged with the Department of Employment and Training. An executive level decision was made in FY83 to establish the Employment Security Commission as the major contractor for the Dislocated Worker Program.

The Department of Employment and Training monitors Employment Security's performance as a service provider under Title III. Several meetings were held between the two agencies during the first months of FY83 to develop a statewide plan for implementing the program. Since that time, the department has assumed what is best described as an oversight role. It provides guidance on policy matters but does not scrutinize every Employment Security funding decision. It depends on the experience of the Employment Security in delivering training services.

In an effort to create a multifaceted approach to the problems of North Carolina's displaced workers, both the Department of Community Colleges and the Department of Commerce received subcontracts from Employment Security to assist in the development of the program. The Department of Community Colleges, an administrative arm for a network of 58 colleges, is primarily responsible for providing institutional training. The Department of Commerce subcontract supports a single staff member and authorizes the Division of Business Assistance to conduct labor market research and coordinate industry involvement.

The state level organization for the Dislocated Worker Program in North Carolina reflects the strong economic development interest on the part of the governor's office. This is further evidenced by North Carolina's New and Expanding Industries Program, which was created to organize efforts to attract new industry to the state. As part of this program, Title III funds are offered as a potential resource to retrain displaced workers for any new industry if it indicates that none of its former employees will be left unemployed in its prior location.

The state attempted to influence service mix through the Governor's Special Service Plan. That document contains a table of planned enrollment and expenditure projections by program activity (see table 6-3).

As indicated in table 6-3, the state planned for more than half of its total Title III funds to be used to provide on-the-job training. The remaining funds were to have been equally divided between institutional training and employment services.

Table 6-3
Title III Enrollment and Expenditure Projections
(Total FY83, TY84, PY84, and Discretionary Funds Equal $7,068,000)

Program activity	Number of enrollees	Funding levels*	Total funding*
Services**	5,850	1,476	20.9
Institutional training	1,700	1,595	22.6
OJT	2,936	3,998	56.6

SOURCE: North Carolina's Governor's Special Service Plan.
*Dollars in thousands.
**This is a catch all service category that includes a job search workshop, employability counseling, and placement services.

The emphasis on OJT is consistent with the economic development interest of the governor's office. OJT involves the private sector and increases job placements. In addition, state plans to enroll more than half of the Title III participants in job search and employability counseling points to a planned emphasis on matching participants with available job opportunities, rather than funding long-term training programs. In fact, rapid job placement through job search and OJT contracts is particularly important in light of a requirement that Employment Security produce a statewide entered employment rate of 72 percent during the transition year and program year 1984.

The Title III contract was awarded to Employment Security on a non-competitive basis in response to the agency's proposal to provide Title III services through its local offices. The Title III coordinator in the Department of Employment and Training cites the following reasons for the selection of Employment Security to operate the program:

- Employment Security has the capacity to effectively and efficiently identify UI eligibles and recipients;

- Employment Security has an excellent track record for conducting intake without audit exceptions; and,

- Employment Security has consistent program procedures across the various local offices.

The importance of the first point should not be understated. North Carolina, like other states has an interest in rapid targeting and placement of those who are receiving benefits from the state UI program supported by a payroll tax on employers. The organization of the program in a job placement agency and the emphasis on job search articulated in the Governor's Special Services Plan indicates the state's program on a statewide basis is that it gives the state maximum flexibility to target resources in any geographical area or on any industry they desire. Equally important is the existing statewide network of Employment Security offices. With training facilities and local staff in place, Employment Security can respond to dislocated worker problems as they surface.

At the beginning of calendar year 1984, each local Employment Security office was authorized to provide Title III services in its area. In addition, the state has targeted plants with "an emerging dislocated worker problem" (plants giving notice of termination). If such a plant happens to be located in an area that does not have a local Employment Security office, the state will set up a local office, as was the case in Hillsborough. Services are primarily directed to workers from the targeted plant. However, state policy requires that services be provided to any person in the area who meets the eligibility criteria with the noted exception of homemakers, farmers, and the self-employed.

The subcontract that Employment Security has with the Department of Community Colleges allows that agency to accomplish two tasks. First, it permits the local offices to enroll dislocated workers in the community college system without having to negotiate a contract for each classroom training enrollee. Second, it helps Employment Security generate the match for the program through the use of state funds provided by the colleges.

Subcontracting with the Division of Business Assistance links it to Employment Security and the Department of Employment and Training to form a task force in charge of identifying local dislocated worker problems. Staff from these three agencies were instrumental in mobilizing a prompt response to the Cone-Mills shutdown. The Division of Business Assistance worked with the personnel staff at the plant to develop a profile of the workers who were laid off. The Orange County Economic Development Agency also assisted local Employment Security staff with initial contact and intake procedures.

There was little private sector involvement in the program and no indication of private sector involvement in the preprogram planning. State officials met with personnel from the Cone-Mills plant before it closed to establish a schedule of events, but the Cone-Mills officials did not involve themselves in program planning. On the implementation level, the only private sector firm involved in service delivery was a professional credit counseling agency. This organization worked directly with Title III referrals to help manage their debts and household budgets.

Due to the lack of union activity in Orange County, there was a total absence of union involvement in the program. The last attempt at unionization was made by the Amalgamated Clothing and Textile Workers Union (ACTWU) in May 1978.

The Eligible Population

Although North Carolina's targeting policy prohibits the exclusion of persons from the program who meet the federal eligibility criteria, the Employment Security office in Hillsborough was opened with the express intent of serving workers displaced by the closing of the Cone-Mills textile plant. According to local staff, "participation was not limited to workers from the Cone-Mills plant, but we have been very careful about serving outsiders because of the large number of Cone-Mills workers that need assistance."

The workers laid off from the mill are closely tied to both plant and community. Attracted by the relatively high entry-level wages the company offered, many of them left high school before completion (33 percent of the enrollees are dropouts) to work at Cone-Mills. The convenient location of the textile mill allowed many employees to walk to and from their job. According to one of the local operators, "Some of the workers walked to work for over fifteen years. . . a number of them don't own cars and some don't even have a valid driver's license."

At the time of the closing, the average wage for the entire plant was $6.75 per hour. This is about equal to the average wage for the textile industry in the Raleigh-Durham SMSA and only $1.31 less than the average wage for the highest paying manufacturing industry in the state.[1] The average entry wage at Cone-Mills was $5.15 per hour. The director of the Durham Employment Security office indicated that this entry wage was significantly higher than the entry wages paid by other companies in the area.

Table 6-4 provides information on the average wage by job title for a sample of 218 of the 550 people who worked at the plant. Table 6-4 also indicates the skill distribution at the Cone-Mills plant. Over 70 percent of the positions involve some type of skill. However, these skills are specific to the textile industry and not easily transferred to other jobs in Orange County. Further, because of increased efforts to mechanize production, many of these skills have become obsolete *within* the textile industry due to introduction of new equipment.

Table 6-4
Average Wage Per Hour by Job Title
for 218 Dislocated Cone-Mills Employees

Job title	Number of workers	Average wage
Cloth inspectors	29	$5.60
Doffers	18	6.85
Loom Fixers	12	8.05
Roving-frame operators	12	6.75
Spinners	30	6.20
Spooler tenders	18	6.15
Weavers	33	7.20
Electricians	4	8.80
Lift-truck operators	5	5.55
Maintenance mechanics	6	8.80
Material handlers	40	5.30
Clerical/payroll clerks	11	6.00

SOURCE: Plant Closing Report, North Carolina Department of Commerce, Business Assistance Division.

Program Services

The Hillsborough Dislocated Worker Project officially opened its doors for group intake on December 27, 1983, three weeks after a letter announcing a March 1984 shutdown had been issued. With the assistance of the Orange County Economic Development Agency, the old courthouse building in downtown Hillsborough was used by Employment Security staff to organize the group intake sessions. Both the local newspaper and the plant ran advertisements which provided instructions for setting up appointments with local staff.

During the first two weeks, the local office held three to four sessions per day. At each session, they talked with approximately 18 Cone-Mills employees. The group intake was used to discuss the Dislocated Worker Program, provide information on how to apply for UI benefits and other services, and encourage workers to stay in the labor force.

After group intake, most of the workers returned to fill out an application form. This form was used in conjunction with a master list from the personnel office of Cone-Mills to determine eligibility. Eligible participants were then enrolled in one of six programs: employment counseling; direct job placement activities; job development; job search skills workshops; GED or community college programs; and on-the-job training.

Participants were not required to enroll in a particular component or a sequence of particular activities. The group intake and enrollment process was used to assess interest in particular components. Following assessment, the local program staff often enrolled participants in a catchall service component which featured job search and employment counseling. Once a participant completed a program, he or she was either terminated or enrolled in another activity. Because of the lack of participant interest in relocating or commuting long distances to work, job placement efforts were focused on businesses in the Durham, Mebane, Chapel Hill, and Burlington areas.

The project has not changed from its original design in any way. Local staff knew that the Hillsborough labor market offered few job opportunities that could match the wage levels paid by Cone-Mills. They were aware of the expanding economy in Orange County and the Raleigh-Durham SMSA; and they also knew that the Cone-Mills employees would not favor traveling outside of Hillsborough to find work. Therefore, their basic strategy was to emphasize the limitations of the Hillsborough labor market while stressing the need to commute to areas where employment opportunities existed. Once this was accomplished, local staff used the range of services discussed earlier to try and match participants with available jobs. Since these factors were considered during the planning stage, major adjustments during the program were not necessary.

The two basic services offered through Hillsborough's classroom training were basic educational courses, and "curriculum programs." The basic educational programs offered remedial or adult basic education services, GED certification courses, and the opportunity to earn a high school diploma. The length of time for these activities was open-ended, determined largely by the participant's ability. Program staff reported longer periods of training for Cone-Mills employees because of their educational deficiencies.

The curriculum programs are either one or two years in length, and offer the opportunity to earn an Associate Degree in several academic and technical fields: digital electronic repair; word processing; teacher's aide; business administration; criminal justice; and nursing. Enrollment in these programs is limited to those participants who meet the entry requirements of the particular institution. There is a need-based payment system in place for participants in classroom training programs. However, staff point out that most participants have second earners in the family who make them ineligible for need-based payments.

OJT slots have been developed for entry level and skilled positions in seven industries or trades. They are: heating and air conditioning; sheet metal work; pipe fitting; construction; electronics; printing; and toy manufacturing. The average length of training is six months.

The job search workshops are designed to improve the job finding techniques of the participants. According to program staff, the participant is made aware of personal strengths and familiarized with proper interview techniques and job application forms. Once the workshop is completed, the job search process becomes self-directed. The staff continue to make employer contacts and provide job listings, but the bulk of the job finding effort falls to the participant. The length of time spent in this activity also varies considerably. Participants are separated from the activity when the workshop ends but remain enrolled in the catch-all service category until they locate a job, leave the labor force, or request to be enrolled in another program activity.

Employability counseling and job search sessions are an integral part of the Title III program in Hillsborough. Although many of the Cone-Mills employees had impressive work histories (some having been employed over 15 years), they were not very knowledgeable about how to locate work.

Equally important is "wage and distance" counseling. The Cone-Mills employees had to come to grips with the reality of working outside Hillsborough and for lower wages. The average wage at Cone-Mills was the second highest among manufacturing industries in the area. Acceptance of a lower wage job was reported to be a tough reality for many participants. One staff member commented, "Even after counseling, participants had to actually experience wage loss or extended unemployment before they accepted what we were saying."

The first service developed was the institutional training program. A learning lab sponsored by the Durham Technical School attracted the early interest of participants primarily because of its convenient location. This thrust lasted about three months. As the program moved through the transition year, staff began to develop a number of OJT contracts with various small businesses and one large contract with an electronics assembly plant. As noted, participants who were not initially enrolled in either of these two components were placed in the catchall service category. Enrollees in this component received job search instruction, employability counseling, job development, and job placement services. The breakdown by service is provided in table 6-5.

Table 6-5
Enrollments in the Hillsborough Title III Program
by Program Activity, February 1985

Program activity	Total number of enrollees*	Percent of enrollees*
Service	315	87.0
OJT	61	16.4
Institutional skills training	50	13.9
Adult Basic Education/GED	51	14.2

SOURCE: Employment Security Commission in Raleigh, North Carolina.

*The figures sum to more than the total number of enrollees (360) and 100 percent because some participants were enrolled in more than one service.

A majority (87 percent) of the participants were enrolled in the catch-all service category at some point during their stay in the program. It was common to provide basic service as an initial intervention before assigning a participant to OJT or institutional training. Local staff indicated that the majority of the participants served through mid-February 1985 favored the job placement activities provided in the services component, rather than long-term retraining programs.

Participant Characteristics

Program staff indicated that over 95 percent of those served in the Hillsborough Title III program were former employees of Cone-Mills. Local staff did not exclude persons who met the federally established criteria, but targeted the program to Cone-Mills workers. This was accomplished by directing intake efforts towards the textile plant workers and by checking each applicant against a personnel list from the plant.

Characteristic data shown in table 6-6 reveal a population that has a slightly higher percentage of blacks (52 percent) than whites, and is mostly female (60 percent). Additionally, 70 percent of the participants were between the ages of 22 and 44; 23 percent were 44 years of age or more; and 33 percent were high school dropouts. The recent labor force attachment of those served is indicated by the high percentage of enrollees who were receiving unemployment insurance benefits upon entering the program (89 percent).

Program Outcomes

Local staff employed two primary job development strategies. First, they had a direct job placement strategy. Through this approach, participants were referred directly to available job openings identified through Employment Security's job development network in Raleigh and Durham, and through phone contacts made by the Hillsborough staff. The second approach was in-house job development, in which staff made daily contact with area employers to inquire about their interest in direct referrals from the program's employability development components or for graduates from the classroom training component.

Table 6-6
Participant Characteristics

Characteristics	Number	Percent
Total participants	360	
Sex		
Male	145	40
Female	215	60
Race		
White	174	48
Black	185	52
Age		
21	26	7
22–44	252	70
45–54	57	16
55 and over	25	7
Education		
School dropout	118	33
High school graduate	242	67
Benefit recipiency		
U.I. claimant	319	89
U.I. exhaustee	10	3
AFDC	9	3
SSI	8	2

On the surface, these placement strategies appear to be very effective. Program data through February 1985 reveal that 225 of 230 participants were terminated into unsubsidized employment. This 98 percent placement rate must be considered with caution. Program data for this same period of time indicate that 360 participants were enrolled in the program. This means that 130 enrolled participants are not considered in the calculation of the entered employment rate through February. Staff indicate that some of these participants are still enrolled in either on-the-job training or classroom training activities. Those not enrolled in these programs are in the catchall service activity. Thus, the actual placement rate could be as low as 63 percent. Final placement figures are not available, because the project staff have been moved to other locations.

Job placements for the 225 participants terminated into unsubsidized employment were in a variety of occupations. Included among those established for participants who were enrolled in the classroom training and services component are: salesperson; cafeteria attendant; cosmetologist; receptionist; dietary aide; garbage collector; clerk typist; audit clerk; janitor; cashier; groundskeeper; security guard; carpenter; dispatcher; electronic repair; and word processor.

The OJT placements were in the construction industry; pipe fitting; heating and air conditioning; sheet metal; electronics assembler; a toy manufacturer; and a printing company.

A surprising finding was that slightly over one-third (34 percent) of all placements were in the textile industry. This suggests two possibilities. The first is that some part of these workers were only frictionally, as opposed to structurally, unemployed. The second (and more likely) possibility is that these workers faced future unemployment as the result of true dislocation in this industry.

The average wage for participants placed was $5.53 per hour. This represents an 86 percent wage replacement rate relative to their pre-layoff average wage. The average termination wage of $5.90 for participants returning to the textile industry is noticeably higher, i.e., a wage replacement rate of 92 percent.

Overall Assessment

There are several important aspects of the Hillsborough Dislocated Worker Program. First, the state gave itself the discretion (via a statewide program organized noncompetitively) and capacity (through its local Employment Security office) to respond rapidly to the problem at Cone-Mills. Staff from the Employment Security office were quick to discern the needs of the target population and plan and implement a strategy for reemployment several months prior to the actual closure of the plant. This made for smooth implementation of the project.

A second important aspect is the targeting of the program to Cone-Mills employees. Had the staff chosen to serve anyone who met the basic eligibility criteria, it is questionable whether the program outcomes would have been as positive. Broadened targeting would bring into the program individuals who could not be easily placed through job search because of insufficient work history and job skills.

The third important aspect was the emphasis that local staff placed on finding immediate employment for those served rather than enrolling the participants in long-term retraining programs. The growing labor market of the surrounding area and the desire of those targeted for immediate placement justifies this approach.

At the same time, the fact that one-third of the placements were back into the textile industry is probably not a positive outcome in the long run. If the textile industry continues to decline, there will be future dislocation. It is therefore possible that reemployment in the textile industry is the nonunion equivalent to unionized employees "waiting for the plant to reopen." While they may be currently employed and receiving income (the nonunion equivalent of supplemental unemployment payments), it is likely that they face long run dislocation.

NOTE

1. This wage comparison is made using 1983 wage data for the electronics industry and 1984 data for the Cone-Mills plant.

7

The Cleveland, Ohio United Labor Agency Dislocated Worker Project

Introduction

The United Labor Agency operates this project in conjunction with the Teamsters Service Bureau; both are union-sponsored social service agencies. The project was funded with FY 1983 discretionary money to provide assessment counseling, job search, classroom training, and on-the-job training to 700 Title III eligible laid-off workers in Cuyahoga County, Ohio.

The Origin of the Project

The Greater Cleveland labor market is defined in this case study as the SMSA (Cuyahoga, Lake, Medina, and Geauga counties) unless otherwise noted. The unemployment rate as of August 1984 was 9 percent. Between June 1978 and June 1982, there were 21,153 plant closings with a loss of 262,314 jobs in the area. A majority of these closings occurred in 1981 and 1982. Types of industries affected included:

Industry	Jobs lost
Manufacturing	72,799
Construction	24,995
Transportation/Utilities	10,297
Wholesale	21,679
Retail	57,712
Service oriented	58,375

111

Obviously, the largest share of those affected went into other jobs but the magnitude of the numbers gives a sense of the lack of stability in this labor market. The labor market is generally depressed, with unemployment rates consistently higher than the national average.

The four-county area has a mixed labor force. As of August 1984, manufacturing constituted 25 percent of the labor force; services, 24 percent; government, 13 percent; and retail/wholesale/insurance/finance/construction, 38 percent. (See table 7-1 for breakdown of nonagricultural employment.)

Table 7-1
Sector Breakdown of Employment
(Nonagricultural)

Nonagricultural jobs	January 1983	August 1983	August 1984
Total	817,300	825,500	831,500
Durable manufacturing	18%	17%	17%
Nondurable manufacturing	8%	8%	8%
Service	23%	24%	24%
Government	14%	14%	NA
Construction, public utilities, retail, wholesale, banking real estate, insurance, finance	37%	37%	38%
Unemployment rate	10.3%	12.5%	9.0%

SOURCE: Ohio Bureau of Employment Services, Monthly Labor Market Report (January 1983 and August 1984).

In the seven-county area of northeast Ohio (Cuyahoga, Portage, Lake, Medina, Lorain, Geauga, and Summit), there are approximately 96,000 Teamster members in 19 locals; 55,000 United Auto Workers members in 48 locals; 28,000 United Steel Workers members in 150 locals; and 17,000 Communication Workers of America in 22 locals.

As of July 1984, and out of a total labor force of approximately 1.2 million, these five large unions have a combined membership that constitutes 17.6 percent of the area labor force; there are additional labor union members in a variety of other unions. The effects of unionization on area wage rates are indicated in table 7-2.

**Table 7-2
Average Hourly Wage Rates
(Nonagricultural)**

Nonagricultural industry	January 1982	January 1983	August 1982	August 1983
Durable manufacturing	$10.10	$10.30	$11.30	$11.96
Nondurable manufacturing	8.37	8.75	8.17	9.39
Service	NA	NA	NA	NA
Government	NA	NA	NA	NA
Construction	13.13	16.10	16.98	19.41
Gas and electric services	11.45	12.01	12.11	13.38
Retail	3.89	4.22	4.39	4.51
Wholesale	8.59	8.83	8.07	8.43
Banking	5.56	6.12	6.17	6.43

SOURCE: Ohio Bureau of Employment Services, Monthly Labor Market Report (August 1984 and January 1983).

State Organization of Title III

The Ohio Bureau of Employment Services (OBES) is the state administrative agency responsible for all JTPA titles. Within OBES, the unit directly responsible is the JTP-Ohio Division, headed by a deputy director who reports directly to the OBES administrator. Thus, JTPA has only indirect access to the governor through the head of OBES, a cabinet position. There are three subdivisions within the JTP-Ohio Division; Planning Services, Field Services, and Administrative Services. Each has functional responsibilities that cut across Titles IIA and III.

The initial step in funding decisions occurs at the staff level within the JTP-Ohio Division, but these decisions progress through a series of vertical steps that end with the governor. Recommendations leaving the division go to a Dislocated Workers Task Force, an advisory group that includes members of the State Job Training Coordinating Council and other experts in the field. The next stage is a recommendation to the Coordinating Council. The final step is the recommendation made by the Council to the governor.

Half of the state's Title III funds are distributed through an RFP process. An additional 35 percent is set aside for an Emergency Retraining Fund which is used to deal with plant closing situations. The remaining 15 percent is a discretionary fund of the governor for special services projects. At no time has the Title III money been distributed through a formula.

The state adopted the language of Section 302 of the Act to define eligibility for the Dislocated Worker Program. The thinking was that the state has so many dislocated workers that it was better to leave the specific definition of eligibility at the local project level.

The state did establish a targeting goal in the RFP portion of the program through the designation of priority target areas. Also, the establishment of the Emergency Retraining Fund, which has 35 percent of the Title III funds, represents a priority to be given to dislocation resulting from specific plant closings. Thus, 70 percent of the money has geographic and/or plant-specific targeting.

It should be noted that the United Labor Agency project was funded through the discretionary fund of the U.S. Secretary of Labor. It also did not have any competition for the state's "nomination" to Washington.

The project was actually submitted under CETA as a multiyear, multimillion dollar project, but was quickly seen by the United Labor Agency as a bridge between CETA and JTPA. When JTPA began, the U.S. Department of Labor (DOL) asked the states for nominations for the discretionary fund. The United Labor Agency sent the state a modified version of what was previously submitted to DOL and, after some negotiation with the state, this became the state's only candidate for discretionary funding. Meanwhile, the Teamsters had been lobbying DOL to get the project approved at the federal level. Given the lobbying effort in Washington, it can be safely said that the state really had little choice in submitting the United Labor Agency proposal. The United Labor Agency subcontract to the Teamsters, a 50-50 split of the money, reflects the important role played by the Teamsters in getting the project funded.

The private sector had no formal involvement in the planning of the project. While attending various community meetings called for other purposes, United Labor Agency representatives would sometimes talk about the project being developed and get informal feedback, but this appears to be the extent of private sector participation in the preapproval period.

At the implementation stage, there is substantial private sector involvement, primarily through the OJT and classroom training components.

The Nature of the Project

The recipient of the grant was the United Labor Agency which, in-turn, subcontracted half of the $1 million grant to the Teamsters Assistance Program, Inc. There are a number of other subcontracts, primarily with organizations providing classroom or specialized training for one or a small number of participants.

The United Labor Agency was incorporated in 1969 as a union-sponsored social service agency. Since 1975, and prior to JTPA, the organization had operated a number of CETA-funded programs, starting with an ex-offenders project. By the late 1970s, it was focusing on projects for laid-off workers. The deputy executive director of the United Labor Agency estimates that it averaged approximately $500,000 a year from CETA projects.

The United Labor Agency is widely connected in the area in a variety of different ways. The executive director of the Agency is treasurer of the local PIC (he is also vice-chairman of the SJTCC). Two SDAs are under the PIC (the City of Cleveland and the balance of Cuyahoga County). The United Labor Agency also operates projects for the SDAs under Title IIA.

The Teamsters Assistance Program, the umbrella agency for the Teamsters Service Bureau, was established in 1977 and within a year was involved in job training programs and received CETA funding for a number of projects. Its focus was on classroom training and its subcontract from the United Labor Agency was its first experience with a comprehensive program. The Teamsters part of the program offered the same services as the United Labor Agency; for some elements, the Teamsters piggybacked their participants onto the United Labor Agency program.

The United Labor Agency had no specific experience with older workers until about two years ago. Its greatest experience lies with the 25-40 age group. However, as more senior persons are being laid off with plant shutdowns, older workers are becoming a more important part of their program.

For this particular project, the principal linkages are with the local community college, various public vocational schools, and private training agencies.

Important linkages are also maintained with a wide range of community service organizations in the area. The largest share of these linkages is maintained through the Information and Referral Service and there have been a small number of agencies used for work experience programs funded by the project.

The United Labor Agency also maintained liaison with state-funded Title III programs in adjacent counties. The United Labor Agency project served residents of Cuyahoga County. During its in-plant orientations, if the United Labor Agency came across persons who worked in Cuyahoga County but lived in Lake or Lorain counties, it would put them in contact with the appropriate Title III project; the reverse arrangements were also made.

The project was implemented basically as proposed, although the contract was modified to reflect the substantial increase in the number of participants in the program. The project was originally scheduled to terminate on September 30, 1984, but was extended three months to December 31, 1984. The principal reason for the extension request was to use unexpended funds which came from a number of sources. These included midyear departure of staff members who were not replaced, lower than anticipated costs in a number of project elements, and some on-the-job and classroom training money that was contracted but not spent because contractors did not fulfill all placement obligations.

As the program progressed, the United Labor Agency found itself with more business than expected. It had originally projected 700 participants for the project, but finally totaled 1,083 participants at its close. When the United Labor Agency submitted a modification request, it increased the projected participant level to match the actual figures it was experiencing. The added participation came through the United Labor Agency, rather than through the Teamster half of the program. Both the United Labor Agency and Teamsters see this as a reflection of the former being better known as a social service agency, and of its reputation for not turning people away.

The structure of the program and the mix of services were not altered over the course of the project. There was, however, some administrative tinkering, i.e., improving the recordkeeping systems and altering some of the forms completed by participants in order to obtain more data.

The Eligible Population

The project originally envisioned a three-year program that would be available to all dislocated workers in the area. As finally approved, it was funded for one year, but provided broad coverage rather than being confined to workers in a single plant or industry. The United Labor Agency took the view that the problem of dislocated workers was too great to permit such selectivity. Also, there are important linkages between the major labor unions in the area which would have made it politically difficult to restrict the project in any way that would seem to favor a particular union.

Despite the union underpinning of the project, approximately two-thirds of the nearly 1,100 participants were listed as nonunion. United Labor Agency officials believe, however, that some of these were union members who were uncertain as to their union status. Of the union participants, the largest share (344) were members of the AFL-CIO and UAW unions. Only 35 participants identified themselves as Teamsters, while another 27 belonged to independent unions.

While the project formally listed 1,083 participants, project benefits were also extended to other members of the household. This reflected the range of possible services available to a participant. For example, the children of a participant might need a certain kind of counseling related to school; or a grandmother living with the participant might need advice on a particular medical problem. These services, provided in part via referral and in part directly by the United Labor Agency, are extended to eliminate or ease the pressures on the participant so they won't be carried over to a new employer.

The largest number of participants tended to be unskilled or semiskilled, although they were employed in highly skilled, highly unionized, industries, which meant that they had enjoyed above average wages for the area. United Labor Agency survey teams found that when they went to plants to be shut down or where there were to be layoffs, the longer term, more highly skilled workers tended to have an extended period of termination income specified in the union contract. These workers tended to have less of an immediate interest in available services, although they might return later when their contract benefits expired. Also, some were close to retirement age and the termination pay would keep them going until the retirement income started. This generally resulted in a greater demand for project services from the relatively less skilled and younger workers with fewer accrued termination benefits.

Broad participation gave rise to an awareness of the program which spread by word of mouth through the community, a major reason why the original projection of 700 participants escalated to nearly 1,100 by the time the project was concluded.

Program Services

The United Labor Agency and the Teamster Service Bureau describe the project as providing comprehensive services from intake to placement. However, the services offered could be considered sequential in nature.

The first stage is *identification* of potential participants through direct contact with union and corporate officials, meetings with laid off and about-to-be-laid-off workers, and media announcements.

A key element of the identification stage for plant closings and layoffs is to hold early meetings with union and company officials as soon as the layoff or plant closing is announced. The first meeting is designed to gather certain demographics on the affected workers and to secure precise information on contractual arrangements relative to severance pay, etc. This is followed by a meeting with the affected workers to explain the services being offered and how community agencies can help them with various social and family services as well as services designed to help get new jobs. This initial identification and counseling stage is organized by a Special Economic Response Team established by the United Labor Agency and United Way Services.

The second stage is *assessment*. Information is obtained from participants on employment and educational history, analysis of adaptability of current skills to new occupations, various health and educational problems that may interfere with job performance, personal needs related to securing a job, e.g., personal hygiene, and human services needs, e.g., daycare during a job search or training program. Some of the assessments are done through formal testing programs conducted through contracts with professional firms.

Following this phase of the assessment, participants meet with counselors to analyze the results and to develop a job plan. At this point, the program sequence usually follows one of three basic program lines: (1) classroom training; (2) OJT; or (3) direct placement. The final step is job placement.

Throughout this sequence, a participant may be directed to community support services, such as detoxification and consumer counseling, and/or become eligible for some direct United Labor Agency services, such as $1 tickets for stage plays, child care, and bus tickets. Also, depending upon the direction taken in the job plan and the duration of any training or educational services, the participant will receive job search training.

The distribution of participants among the direct program services was a follows:

Total number of participants	1,083
Assessment	738
Job search	773
Classroom training	157
Basic education	1
OJT	133
Work experience	9

These are not mutually exclusive categories since a person counted for assessment may also appear in the training and job search categories later in the program. There were more than 300 persons counted as participants who never went through the assessment stage. Assessments are counted only if the United Labor Agency or Teamsters spent money to have a participant undertake the various assessment tests. For various reasons, individuals frequently might not be given the battery of tests, but move directly to some kind of counseling or support service.

There were 20 firms utilized in OJT. A total of 133 placements were made in occupations ranging from general clerical to insurance sales. The two largest single placements were for nine press helpers in a steel company and 36 water meter installers in a commercial metering firm.

A total of 157 participants received classroom training that included: general business skills; air conditioning and refrigeration; cement masonry; data entry and computer programming; secretarial/word-processing; sewing; floral design; vending machine repair; and construction and building weatherization. Program durations ranged from three weeks to six months; the average duration was approximately three months. In several instances, training programs funded from other sources and with which participants had been involved, or ones in which they were already enrolled when this project began, were adopted into the Title III project, making it possible to complete a previously initiated program. This kind of overlap also provided some early headcounts.

Industry and occupational classifications of overall placements include the following:

supervisory positions;
labor agency;
steel;
automotive;
retail;
heating and cooling;
restaurant/bar;
air freight transportation;
commercial metering;
laborer;
insurance;
teaching;
security guard;
hospital;
transportation/delivery;
building trades;
technical/computer programming;
office/clerical;
construction;
sales;
shipping and receiving; and
drafting.

While the occupations are varied, there were concentrations of placements in the office, laborer, commercial metering, trades, sales, security, and retail fields.

Various kinds of counseling are central to this project. One United Labor Agency staff member said, "These people are afraid," and require considerable handholding.

The first stage of counseling occurs at *intake* when various United Labor Agency, Teamster, and community service persons describe generally the range of services available, involving not only the training programs but also the various support services that are available in the community.

The next major counseling step comes after the various skills and educational tests have been given. This involves individual meetings with a United Labor Agency or Teamster job counselor who works out a job plan, which may or may not involve OJT or classroom training.

Counseling also takes place in the job search workshop where participants are taught how to look for a job and provided information on personal appearance, the kinds of information to give to prospective employers, what kinds of things to withhold, etc. In some cases, persons go directly from the intake to the job search stage, while others do not enter job search until other forms of counseling or training are completed.

Counseling also takes place through the information and referral service which guides participants to support services provided through various community service agencies. These can include consumer counseling, alcoholism programs, rental assistance, etc. The linkage here is the working relationships between the United Way (which provides some of the United Labor Agency funding) and other community service organizations. This project also provided some money for direct United Labor Agency services, such as child care and bus tickets. Support service counseling can take place at any point in the process.

Given the high percentage of participants who do not receive OJT, classroom training, or work experience services, it is safe to say that counseling in its various forms is the foundation of the project.

Program Participants

When the initial release about the project was made to the media, there were immediately about 2,500 phone calls. A very rough estimate is that about one-third of these came from Title IIA eligibles. Some came to the orientation but left when they learned they wouldn't get any CETA-type income support. There were some Title IIA eligibles who also were classified as dislocated workers and who were interested in jobs and participated in the Title III project.

With regard to differences between workers eligible for Title IIA and Title III, one United Labor Agency staff member said, "A world of difference. The economically disadvantaged of Title IIA have historically been on welfare and are program hoppers. They come for supportive services, but they are not interested in working. They will respond to every request, but when it comes time to look for a job, they don't come back."

By general contrast, the Title III participants were persons who have worked, and were both eligible for and could benefit from the project. The characteristics of the participants are indicated in table 7-3.

Program Outcomes

There are four basic placement processes operated through this project:

(1)   Job order placements. These job openings are developed by Job Developers who visit potential employers. They reach out beyond the Cuyahoga County project area;

(2)   Self-directed placement. Following participation in the Job Search Workshop, these persons go out seeking their own jobs using the information gained at the Workshop to get through the employer's door;

(3)   Placement following classroom training. Training contractors have a built-in performance standard. They must contractually agree that they will place at least 60 percent (the state standard) of persons undertaking the classroom training. In cases where training schools will not agree to performance-based contracts, the United Labor Agency will go to contract only if the verifiable average placement rate of the school's trainees exceeds the performance standard;

Table 7-3
Enrollment and Participation Characteristics for the Period
October 1983 through December 1984

Characteristics	Overall	Percent
Total participants	1,083	
Total terminations	991	
Entered employment	445	45
Other positive terminations	458	86
Other terminations	88	9
Sex		
Male	666	67
Female	325	33
Age		
14–15	NA	
16–19	20	2
20–21	37	4
22–44	683	69
45–54	169	17
55 and over	82	8
Education		
School dropout	199	20
School (H.S. or less)	4	*
High school graduate or more	788	80
Race		
White	392	40
Black	574	58
Hispanic	17	2
Native American	5	*
Asian	3	*
Employment barriers		
Limited English	19	2
Handicapped	6	*
Offender	—	
Other	—	
Benefit recipiency		
U.I. claimant	235	24
U.I. exhaustee	—	
Public assistance (GA)	—	
AFDC	—	
Youth AFDC	—	
Labor force status (prior 26 weeks)		
Unemployed 1–14 weeks	—	
Unemployed 15 or more weeks	977	99

*Less than .5 percent.

(4)   OJT. Self-defined placement process.

The official direct placement rate for the project was 45 percent. This was below the state standard, but that standard had not been established at the time the project was approved. Also, the project was funded from the secretary's discretionary fund and not from state Title III funds for which the standard is applied.

The United Labor Agency and Teamsters feel quite good about their various placement channels and regard them as quite effective. The overall rate of 45 percent obscures several important factors. One factor concerns the large intake of the program. The original proposal contemplated 700 participants, but this ended up being 1,083. The program director noted that, "We didn't cream. We took everyone eligible." This meant taking in a number of persons who were not educationally prepared for a training program and referring them to other service agencies in the area that could address their particular problems. In some of these cases, the United Labor Agency and Teamsters did help them get minimum wage jobs, but they were not counted as a placement. The state has a performance standard of $5.25 an hour for a job placement. Those who were counted as direct placements were only those who met that standard. According to the United Labor Agency, if the minimum wage referrals were counted, the overall placement would have exceeded the 60 percent state standard. Officials point to a positive termination rate of 91 percent. While the state was not happy with the large overrun on intake, the United Labor Agency responds, "We are a social service agency. We are here to help people. In fact, we were able to help more people with the same amount of money."

Relocation is a very minor part of the project. Any relocation assistance is informational through AFL-CIO offices across the country. No payments are involved.

Aside from the measured 45 percent placement rate, which is biased downward, other outcome measures are a cost per placement of $829 for participants who went through OJT and $906 for participants in classroom training. This reflects the short-term nature of the project and its emphasis on counseling, assessment, and use of other community services.

The average wage at entry was $7.12 and the wage at placement was $6.32, for a wage replacement rate of 89 percent. The wage replacement rate is probably raised by the number of lower-wage participants from the hospital industry who were placed at wage rates above their preprogram wage.

Because of the way the data were maintained and assembled, some data are not directly comparable or complete and care should be taken in any efforts to compare these numbers with other jurisdictions.

The Teamsters portion of the project had an actual placement of 261 persons. Their data showed a preproject average wage of $7.71 an hour; the postproject average was $6.32 an hour, a drop of 28 percent.

The United Labor Agency placements totaled 207 persons. The preproject average wage was $6.38 an hour; postproject $6.11, a 96 percent wage replacement rate. The United Labor Agency broke down its pre-and postproject wage levels into OJT and classroom training groups (total participants in each, not just placements). For 63 classroom training participants, the preproject average hourly wage was $5.40 an hour; postproject was $5.91. For 73 OJT participants, the preproject wage was $4.40 an hour; postproject was $6.18. In both cases, there was an increase in wages. Had only the placements been calculated, the wage levels before and after would have been somewhat higher.

The *total* number of placements for which data were available was 468 persons. The preproject average was $7.12; postproject was $6.32 an hour, a wage replacement rate of 89 percent. The total placement (468 persons) is slightly below the 486 official total because some persons were placed in jobs based on commissions or piece work.

The Teamster wages tend to be higher because their participants generally had come from higher paying jobs and were able to get somewhat better placements.

The cost per placement figures ($829 and $906) are not actually per placement, but per person getting OJT or classroom training. In the case of OJT, the per person costs are close to being the same ($829) since the OJT program virtually coincided with placements; for classroom training, the cost per placement would actually be higher than the $906 since not all persons undergoing classroom training ended up with a job.

Overall Assessment

The major constraint on the operation and perhaps long-term effectiveness of the project appeared to be the one-year funding limit. This was a particular handicap for some classroom training possibilities. By the time the project was running and training contracts were negotiated, the actual time left for training was substantially less than one year. Also, many laid-off workers have various contractual supplementary unemployment benefit arrangements that make it financially possible to delay entry into the training process. By the time the economic realities set in, the project is close to ending.

The short-term duration of the project also constrains the kinds of training that can be undertaken. For example, training programs for repair of high tech machinery cannot be undertaken although such training would provide considerable employment potential in this area.

Another constraining factor is the lack of stipends during the training period. The longer the training, the more this becomes a hardship on persons who would benefit from the training. They are unable to sustain themselves and their families for an extended period of time without some kind of income support. The United Labor Agency does try to find part-time work, but in many cases, it is not enough.

Overall, this particular project was appropriate to the large need and diverse kinds of dislocated workers in the area. But the opportunities for both the dislocated workers and the skill needs of the area may have been affected by the one-year limit to the project. For policy purposes, it might be worth considering ways of encouraging multiyear projects.

8
The Houston Community College-Texas Employment Commission Dislocated Worker Project

Introduction

The Houston Dislocated Worker Project is operated by the Houston Community College (HCC) and the Texas Employment Commission (TEC). The project, funded out of transition year 1984 Title III funds, provides services to dislocated workers in Harris County and the City of Houston. Job search, classroom training and on-the-job training were planned for 650 workers laid off from the steel, shipbuilding, oil field machinery and equipment, and industrial chemical industries.

The Origin of the Project

Despite the perception of Texas, and Houston in particular, as prototypical of the sunbelt, the unemployment rate in the Houston Metropolitan Area in September 1983 was 10 percent (61st out of the nation's 244 SMSAs); and for the City of Houston itself, 11 percent. At the same time the State of Texas posted the 18th highest unemployment rate among the states (8.6 percent). The relatively poor economies of Texas and Houston were largely attributable to problems in energy-related industries both at home and abroad, e.g., Mexico.

A survey conducted by the Texas Employment Commission in mid-1983 showed that except for banking, real estate, services, and government, all other industries in the Houston area had experienced a sizable decline in total employment over the past year. The industries most severely affected were those manufacturing oil field machinery and equipment, supplying those manufacturers, or engaged in oil and gas drilling and extraction. This, in turn, carried over into the construction industry, which was also characterized by substantial layoffs. An analysis of insured unemployed workers in the Houston area showed that 60 percent were from the mining, construction, and manufacturing industries.

Indicative of the employment trends in petrochemical-related industries in the Houston area in 1983 were the closing of an Armco steel mill complex, which put about 2,500 workers out of jobs, and layoffs at Gulf, Superior, and Exxon Oil Company headquarters, Cameron Iron and Brown & Root. Other major nonpetrochemical-related layoffs were of employees of Continental Airlines and Weingarten's, a large grocery store chain which was closed and sold.

In summary, in spite of the fact that the Houston economy had been described as fairly diversified, the employment problems which emerged in 1982 and 1983 revealed the true extent to which its labor market is dependent upon the development, production, refining, and transportation of oil and petrochemical products, and the manufacture of machinery and equipment related to the oil industry.

A local labor market demand study, conducted by the University of Houston Center for Public Policy in spring 1984, identified the major long-term growth occupations, ranked from highest to lowest, as secretaries/typists; clerks; tellers; nursing staff; truck drivers; plumbers and plumber apprentices; data entry; air conditioning repair and installation; printers; electricians; auto mechanics; concrete workers; heavy equipment operators; automobile parts sales; medical lab technicians; dental assistants; carpenters; security guards; and exterminators.

Another survey, done in May 1984 by the Texas Employment Commission, reported the major occupational shortages in the Houston area at that time were for electronic technicians, mechanical engineers, cashiers, clerks, housekeepers, cooks, food service workers, security guards, waiters and waitresses, auto mechanics, air conditioning mechanics, carpenters, carpet layers, plumbers, apartment maintenance workers, auto body repairers, neon tube benders, forklift operators, material handlers, service station attendants, sign painters, stationary engineers, and truck drivers (see table 8-1).

State Organization of Title III

The Texas JTPA Program is directly administered by the Training and Employment Development Division of the Texas Department of Community Affairs (TDCA). TDCA has a unique, direct relationship to the governor's office since it is the only major state agency that does not have a board or commission functioning in a policy development and program oversight role. As a consequence, TDCA is viewed as "the governor's agency."

Within the governor's office, there is also a small employment and training section in the Office of Planning, which works with the JTPA staff in the Training and Employment Development Division of TDCA. It primarily offers input on policy decisions and serves in a coordinating, or liaison role with the private sector members of the State Job Training Coordinating Council and local Private Industry Councils (PICs) across the state.

All Title III projects are competitive demonstration projects to service delivery areas (SDAs). The aim of the Title III program in Texas is to provide relief to targeted areas of the state with serious worker dislocation problems. The bulk of the funded Title III projects have provided various types of job search assistance to aid workers in targeted industries in these areas. A politically important element of the Title III program, particularly from the governor's perspective, is a portion of funds set aside for emergencies (unforeseen layoffs and/or plant closures). This emergency fund has given the governor the flexibility to respond quickly to major economic crises which have hit key industries in areas without a diversified economic base, e.g., the petrochemical industry in the Beaumont-Port Arthur area in program year 1984.

Table 8-1
Heavy Demand Occupations (Houston Area)

Ranking of specific occupations with long-term potential (April 1984)[1]	Categories of specific occupations in demand (May 1984)[2]
Secretaries-typists	Professional, technical & managerial
	Electronic technician
Clerks	Mechanical engineer
	Clerical and sales
Tellers	Cashier
	Clerk, general
Nursing staff	Insurance sales
	Retail sales
Truck drivers	Secretary
	Word processor
Plumbers and plumber apprentices	Service
	Cleaner, housekeeping
Data entry	Cook
	Food service workers
Air conditioning repair and installation	Guard
	Waiter/waitress
Printers	Machine trades
	Air conditioning mechanic
Bookkeepers	Auto mechanic
	Structural work
Electricians	Apartment maintenance workers
	Auto body repairer
Auto mechanics	Carpenter
	Carpet layer
Concrete workers	Neon tube bender
	Plumber
Heavy equipment operators	Miscellaneous
	Forklift operator
Automobile parts salespersons	Material handlers
	Service station attendant
Medical lab technicians	Sign painter
	Stationary engineer
Dental assistants	Truck driver
Carpenters	
Security personnel	
Pest exterminators	

1. University of Houston Center for Public Policy.
2. Texas Employment Commission.

TDCA allocated Title III funds for transition year 1984 and program year 1984 through an RFP process to targeted geographical areas of the state with serious structural worker dislocation problems, as opposed to areas merely suffering from cyclical downturns. The criteria used by the state in making funding decisions included: quality of the proposed project; commitment and coordination of the public and private sectors; experience and expertise of the staff; past track record of the proposed service provider; the extent to which both target industries (dislocation) and growth industries (hosts) were identified; provision for local matching funds; and evidence of community support and participation.

The state did not establish statewide Title III eligibility criteria, leaving such decisions to the discretion of program operators. The state did target specific geographical areas, namely those with high unemployment, layoffs and plant closures (Gulf Coast, East Texas, Border). In most cases, this targeting was on industries, but industry-specific requirements were never made part of any statewide eligibility criteria.

The state influenced the mix of services for its Title III programs through its structuring of the Requests for Proposals (RFPs). From the start, it appears the state basically, although informally, acknowledged that the most pressing need of the majority of dislocated workers was job search assistance. For transition year 1984 funds, the state issued one RFP ($2.1 million) which called for providers to deliver both job search and training, retraining, and relocation services. Another RFP ($225,000) was issued to select service providers to deliver only job search, counseling, and referral. In program year 1984, all projects were based on this two-tier model.

There were no specific service requirements for Title III operators in the Governor's Special Services Plan for the Transition Year. As stated, the "projects will provide job search assistance, training, retraining, and relocation assistance to workers dislocated by structural changes in the economy." The program year 1984 and program year 1985 Governor's Special Services Plan specifies only that "new demonstration projects will continue to use the project design employed by transition year projects which entails: (1) serving the structurally unemployed with limited opportunities for reemployment in high unemployment areas; and (2) utilizing the two-tier (job search assistance coupled with intensive classroom training/retraining) design with 'host' firms."

Initially, the state on recommendation of the governor, had planned to spread Title III money around the state in each successive year of funding by changing the targeted geographical areas. However, this strategy was abandoned when it came time to issue RFPs for program year 1984 because it was apparent that some of the initially targeted areas, e.g., Houston, still had high numbers of dislocated workers even as the rest of the state began to recover from the recession. The JTPA staff recommended, and the State Job Training Coordinating Council approved, refunding for transition year 1984 Title III projects, including the project covered in this study.

The Nature of the Project

The Houston Community College-Texas Employment Commission (HCC-TEC) transition year 1984 project was originally designed to serve 650 workers laid off from the oil field machinery and equipment, shipbuilding, steel, and industrial chemical industries by offering job search and placement assistance as well as classroom and on-the-job training to eligible participants. The project fit in well with the needs of the local labor market since these were the industries hit hardest by changes in the petrochemical market and its technology.

By June 1984, the end of the transition year, the unemployment rate in the Houston area remained at the 10 percent level, still higher than the statewide rate of 8.5 percent. The same industries were still experiencing problems so that the program year 1984 HCC-TEC Title III project targeted dislocated workers from these industries as well as construction and the oil and gas extraction industries.

Once the state identified the geographical areas to be targeted for Title III demonstration projects in transition year 1984, and when TDCA had issued an RFP, training officials from Houston Community Col-

lege approached administrators in local offices of the Texas Employment Commission who handle special services to talk about the possibility
of submitting a joint proposal. The two agencies have a long history
of participation in federal employment and training programs as joint
ventures. The eventual proposal called for HCC to provide the classroom
training portion of the project; TEC would handle job search assistance
and on-the-job training, as well as intake, eligibility determination, and
placement. The HCC-TEC proposal was one of four submitted to TDCA
from the Houston/Harris County SDAs, one of the five geographical
areas targeted for Title III assistance. It was ultimately selected using
the criteria described earlier.

The recipient of the Title III grant is actually Houston Community
College, which in turn subcontracts with the Texas Employment Commission, which in turn subcontracts with a number of other agencies
for program operations such as Career Circles, Inc., which provides
skills assessment, motivational training, career counseling and planning, and Neighborhood Centers, Inc., which provides day care services for participants.

The following firms are OJT subcontractors of TEC:

Transition year 1984	Program year 1984
Tanco, Inc.	Comet Rice
G & H Tool and Die Company	Airco/McMorrough, Inc.
Goins Engine Machine Shop	Container Maintenance
Espey, Huston & Assoc., Inc.	Services, Inc.
Cooper Valve Co.	Kent Process Control, Inc.
Metropolitan Transit Authority	Northern Engineering
	International Company
	Espey, Huston & Assoc., Inc.

Both HCC and TEC have long histories of participation in special
employment and training programs, as do the individuals administering the Title III project from both agencies. This includes experience
with programs for adults. For example, when HCC was created in the
early 1970s, it absorbed the adult training portion of Houston Indepen-

dent School District. TEC, being part of the state Employment Services system, naturally has always dealt with experienced and older workers.

As noted above, this project is an integral part of the employment and training system in the Houston area, since it is jointly administered by two of the key actors in the system, i.e., the community college and the Employment Service. The other linkages (with SDAs, unions and employers) are more indirect. For example, the TEC JTPA project manager attends meetings of the Private Industry Councils of both SDAs serviced by this project (Houston, balance of Harris County) and sends monthly reports to administrators of each SDA. In addition, TEC and HCC representatives sit on both local PICs. In terms of union linkages, the TEC and HCC JTPA staffs include individuals who were formerly activists in local unions. They maintain close contact with the unions and have been instrumental in encouraging participants of relevant unionized groups, as in the closing of Weingarten's Grocery chain. HCC regularly solicits input from the local union community and has union representatives on its curriculum committees. Both TEC and HCC also have staff whose formal job responsibility is to involve the private sector in their programs, including JTPA.

To date, private sector involvement has not been as extensive as the program administrators would like. Its involvement has been through traditional mechanisms at both HCC and TEC. For example, at HCC, private sector representatives sit on the college's various training program curriculum committees and are constantly involved in updating training requirements in light of local labor market conditions. At TEC, the private sector's primary involvement has been through its use of regular TEC services which produces labor market occupational demand data helpful to JTPA administrators and trainers.

The JTPA project manager at TEC did note that she carefully monitors the business community for proposed mergers or sales and directly contacts company officials to determine if layoffs are anticipated. If so, she informs them of the JTPA Title III program and offers to come to the business to recruit participants.

Union involvement has largely been solicited by TEC JTPA staff and, in general, the unions have cooperated. For example, when the heavily-unionized Weingarten's Grocery chain was closed, a TEC JTPA staff member contacted union officials who agreed to set up a seminar for HCC-TEC to describe the Title III program and recruit participants. Likewise, when Continental Airlines was dissolved, its union was contacted and sent 25 to 30 members to the HCC-TEC program

The only negative reaction of unions to the JTPA transition year 1984 Title III program came from the Metropolitan Transit Authority union. It held up TEC's proposed OJT contract with MTA to train entry level diesel mechanics because it wanted the money to be used to upgrade jobs of employees already on board.

The Target Population. As noted earlier, an analysis of the local economic conditions determined that the targeted industries would be oil field machinery and equipment manufacturing, shipbuilding and repair, steel, petroleum refining and industrial chemical processing and construction, and the oil and gas extraction industries. The initial plan projected the following:

- 84 percent of the participants completing the program should be male;
- 77 percent 22-44 years of age;
- 26 percent college graduates; and
- 54 percent nonwhite.

The actual figures were:

- 81 percent male;
- 78 percent 22-44 years of age;
- 25 percent college graduates; and
- 63 percent nonwhites.

Initially, the majority of the participants were white-collar workers from Houston's petrochemical corporate headquarters, e.g., Exxon, Superior. These corporations adopted layoff strategies which focused on middle management positions. However, midway through the funding period, the sale and closure of Weingarten's Grocery store chain produced a number of blue-collar dislocated workers.

Eligibility Criteria. To be eligible for participation, all workers from the targeted industries had to be unemployed and eligible for, receiving, or having exhausted their unemployment insurance benefits. Additionally, eligible workers had to meet one or more criteria: their job or function was permanently eliminated; they were unlikely to return to their previous industry or occupation; they faced limited reemployment opportunities in the Houston SMSA labor market; they possessed obsolete skills due to technological change; or their age served as a barrier to reemployment.

TEC was responsible for recruiting and determining eligible participants. Potential participants were pulled from the TEC computer or walk-in applications by claim status and occupational code. A local TEC official then called the individual to ask if he/she was interested in participating in the program. If the individual replied positively, he/she was asked to go to the central project service center to determine eligibility and the type of assistance and skills needed to secure employment in stable, productive jobs offering a minimum long-term wage loss.

Types of Assistance Offered. All participants took part in a job search workshop which, on the average, lasted three weeks. These workshops were for groups of 12 to 15 participants and were conducted by either the Texas Employment Commission or Career Circles, Inc. Job search activities included skills assessment tests and motivational courses as well as job search skills and strategies such as resume writing, interviewing, job inquiry, identification of the hidden, or unadvertised, job market, etc.

If job search activities were unsuccessful, the participant was then sent through either classroom training, conducted by Houston Community College, or on-the-job training, arranged for the individual by TEC. During the nine-month period, 24 percent of the participants received classroom training; 7 percent were placed in OJT.

If the participant entered classroom training, he or she normally attended classes six hours a day for 6 to 16 weeks, depending on the skill covered by the course. The average time spent in classroom training was 12 weeks. Occupational training programs at the college level were identified as high demand by JTPA personnel at HCC with input from business executive advisory groups. Occupational training programs viewed as having the most potential for dislocated workers in the Houston area were air conditioning and refrigeration, computer maintenance, computer command automotive electronic technology, diesel mechanics, secretarial and clerical (especially word processing), and computer-aided drafting. In some cases, participants were put into the regular courses offered by HCC. In other cases, courses were designed just for JTPA Title III participants. For example, a course was created for cashiers laid off from Weingarten's Grocery chain to help them find bank teller jobs. The course offerings and scheduling were very flexible and tailored to the individual participant as carefully as possible.

OJT subcontracts were developed by TEC to aid participants for whom no appropriate classroom training programs existed. The bulk of the OJT contracts were for entry level wages around $6.00 per hour. Those paying considerably higher were usually highly specialized sales jobs, i.e., $13.47 per hour for a chemical equipment sales engineer. In fact, one of the most successful strategies used by TEC personnel was to encourage white-collar participants to go into sales in fields related to their area of expertise.

With the exception of the Metropolitan Transit Authority which subcontracted to train 10 bus drivers and 21 diesel mechanics, most OJT contracts were for training 1 or 2 participants. Individuals who were not employed following their classroom training or OJT were sent back to TEC for an additional intensive placement effort, lasting up to two weeks.

Supportive Services. All participants were offered and accepted a transportation subsidy. Participants were paid $5 per day by TEC while involved in job search activities. Those involved in classroom training were paid $10 per week to defray transportation costs. Child care services were available from Neighborhood Centers, Inc. under contract with TEC, and from HCC. Six percent of the participants took advantage of child care suppport services.

The service sequence for participants was somewhat fixed (job search followed by classroom training or OJT, then intensive placement activities). However, the time spent within each activity varied for individual participants.

All participants receive job search assistance which, on the average, lasts three weeks but may last up to five weeks if an individual's counselor feels he/she is close to getting a job. It should be noted that one objective of the HCC-TEC program is early reemployment. The plan was for nearly 70 percent of the participants to be employed within eight weeks of entry. The assumption was that most of the participants had been good, faithful employees, some on the job for 10 years or more, who were simply victims of a changing economy. It was anticipated that most had not been on the job market for years and simply did not know how to go about looking for a job or how to repackage their skills to make them saleable in the Houston labor market.

Program designers expected most participants would be psychologically devastated and in need of motivational counseling to restore their self-confidence as quickly as possible. Consequently, during the first week, participants were put through a series of confidence-building activities, including skills and aptitude tests, skills assessment, and the *What Color is Your Parachute?* exercise. Counselors worked with each individual and developed an employability plan. Individuals with similar needs were then assigned to group job search workshops, usually composed of 12 to 15 participants. Trainers (either TEC or Career Circles, Inc., in transition year 1984; TEC only in program year 1984) worked on polishing the participants' job search skills; resume writing, interviewing, phone and in-person inquiries, dress, and monitoring the local, regional, and national job markets, including the hidden market. Individuals had access to a Resource Center where want ads from local, regional, and national publications, professional and occupational guides, the TEC job bank, and a job leads board were available for their daily perusal. Participants were required to make at least five contacts per day. They attended two classes a day, totaling three hours, and had the rest of the day to look for jobs.

Another attractive feature of the Resource Center was that it served as a temporary office for these individuals, complete with a secretary to type their resumes and letters and several typewriters and phones, a phone message board, a copy machine, and office supplies for their use.

Participants praised the job search assistance portion of the program. They were particularly impressed with the group job search approach. One former participant reported it was extremely helpful to "see other people at the same professional level in the same boat and to know that you're not the only one having trouble finding a job." He was also appreciative of the quality of the training personnel and the Resource Center.

The original projection was that 38 percent of the participants would need only job search assistance to get a job. Most of those still unemployed after four weeks of job search assistance were referred to either classroom or OJT training. During the transition year, 24 percent went through classroom training. HCC, in designing the training programs for Title III participants, first determined the occupational demands in the area (see table 8-1) and then determined whether a training program was already available or could be designed to fall within the 12-week training time frame. The training programs selected are reported in table 8-2. Occasionally, students were counseled to take regular college credit HCC course offerings. The more common practice was to place participants in existing training programs characterized as "open entry-open exit" with monthly enrollment cycles. Another common strategy was to create classes specifically for the participants when demand warranted it; at HCC 12 persons are sufficient to create a class. The latter strategy was followed in creating programs in computer maintenance, computer-aided drafting, computer skills upgrading, and bank tellering. The overall goal was to put together a group of classes that made a *full-time* training package, minimum of 6 hours per day; 30 hours per week, for 6 to 16 weeks. The original proposal also called for the participant to spend the remainder of his/her training period at an actual work site, 40 hours per week, while only spending 4 hours per week in the classroom. This idea was abandoned because of the Houston job market. Employers did not feel they had to participate in a training program to get good people.

Table 8-2
Classroom Training Options for JTPA Title III Participants
Houston Community College

Category/type	Category/type
Office occupations	Computer/electronics
Secretary	Computer maintenance technology
Clerk	Electronics technician
Accounting clerk	Computer programming
Word processor	Radio/TV repair
Typist	CAD
Tourist/travel trades	
Bank teller	Food services
Office manager	Catering
Receptionist	Food service
Data entry	Cook
Data processing	Bartender
Press operator	Restaurant manager
	Waiter/waitress
Auto services	Hotel/motel occupations
Auto mechanic	Floral occupations
Diesel mechanic	
Auto body repairs	Miscellaneous[1]
Heavy vehicle maintenance	Sales
	Transportation
Building services	Delivery
Air conditioning mechanic	Real estate appraisal
Apartment maintenance	Cosmetology
Apartment management	
Security	
Electrical wiring technology	
Appliance repair	

1. Used only in unusual situations since many of these involve longer periods of training than are available under the Title III program.

The HCC-TEC project had no eligibility requirements for entry into the classroom training program. When the participant was referred to HCC, he/she came with a resume in hand, and his or her Birkman Test scores. One of five counselors was assigned to the individual to discuss training options.

HCC took all referrals from TEC. However, they did send back about 10 percent, those individuals for whom no meaningful training program could be designed. According to the HCC JTPA director, the vast majority of those sent to HCC were college-educated, mid-level draftsmen, designers, or engineers. They were usually in their 40s. There were also a significant number of foreigners, particularly Middle Easterners, most laid off from petrochemical companies.

The most difficult to deal with were the engineers who had unrealistic views of the status of their profession and refused to look at their layoff as anything but a temporary phenomenon. According to the counselors, they were extremely difficult to counsel because they had no desire to change careers or refocus their skills in more employable occupations. As the figures in table 8-3 show, the majority of those sent to HCC in the transition year went through the office occupation, data processing, computer technology and maintenance, air conditioning and refrigeration, engineering technology, vehicle maintenance and repair, or real estate training programs. The proportion of HCC trainees placed was 70 percent. Another 5 percent of the trainees enrolled in school following their classroom training.

As noted earlier, most OJT subcontracts were developed by TEC to aid participants for whom no appropriate classroom training program could be designed by HCC. The bulk of the OJT contracts were for entry-level wages around $6.00 per hour. Employers who participated were reimbursed for 50 percent of the wages paid to a trainee for up to 20 weeks. The understanding was that trainees were to be hired immediately and receive all benefits provided other employees. Most OJT contracts were arranged with small companies willing to train machinists and equipment operators. The largest single OJT contract was with the Metropolitan Transit Authority which agreed to train bus drivers and diesel mechanics. TEC personnel responsible for arranging OJT contracts reported they had the most success with small companies, particularly if they could personally meet with the company owner. They reported little luck in dealing with personnel offices or large companies.

Table 8-3
Enrollment in HCC Classroom Training Courses
Transition Year

Training course	Number of participants with all/part of training in course
Air conditioning and refrigeration	16
Mechanical engineering technology	21
Electronic engineering technology	13
Industrial electricity	7
Aviation maintenance technology	1
Stationary engineer	1
Heavy vehicle maintenance	8
Auto mechanics	6
Diesel mechanics	1
Welding	1
*Computer maintenance	7
*Computer aided drafting	22
*Computer skills seminar	11
Data processing	17
Word processing	1
Office occupations	44
Business occupations	2
GED/typing	2
Business technology	1
Travel and tourism	3
Accounting	2
Technical communications	1
*Financial management (bank teller)	13
Human resources management	9
Industrial & retail sales and marketing	1
Commercial art	1
Interior design	1
Upholstery	1
Real estate	11
Real estate tax appraisal	5
Cosmetology	3
Cook/chef	5

*Courses designed specifically for Title III participants.

Finally, individuals who still had not found a job following their classroom training or OJT, were then afforded additional, intensive placement services for one to four weeks. TEC officials were assigned to help each participant find a job. Usually they were given priority for TEC job bank listings. Thirty-nine percent of the participants, much higher than the 24 percent initially projected, went through the intensive placement exercise.

As already noted, counseling for both job search skills and wage expectations is a very important component of this project. It is an integral, almost daily, activity in job search assistance. Participants are also counseled as they enter classroom training and develop their training plan. They are assigned to a counselor who specializes in the broad training area which includes the specific training program(s) in which they are interested. Likewise, they interact with a TEC counselor/monitor if they are being sent through OJT. Finally, they receive intensive daily counseling if they ultimately must go through the final program activity, intensive placement. At each step, participants are served by counselors assigned to help them. In other words, counseling assignments are *not* random or on a first come, first served basis. The goal is high quality personal interaction between a counselor who knows the participant's interests, skills, goals, and needs and the participant. Most of the participants felt that counselors were quite good, and *honest* about the job market and their potential for employment in various capacities at certain wage levels.

Program Participants

Most of the participants during the transition year were midcareer types laid off from the oil field machinery and equipment manufacturing, shipbuilding and repair, steel, petroleum refining and industrial chemical processing and construction, and the oil and gas extraction industries, the targeted industries, as well as some food-related industries, (Weingarten's Grocery store chain, and Bama Foods). Most were male (81 percent), in their late thirties or forties (78 percent). Nearly two-thirds (63 percent) were nonwhites. One-fourth (25 percent) were college graduates. Most of the college graduates had held middle management or professional positions in petrochemical related corporate headquarters.

All eligible participants from the targeted industries were enrolled. Recall that the process for recruiting participants was for TEC to contact individuals who appeared eligible, namely, in the correct industry codes, and ask them if they were interested in participating. The recruitment process stopped when the class was full. The HCC-TEC project actually was able to serve 855 participants on funding which had originally been planned to serve 650.

Program Outcomes

Interviews with participants in the TEC job search program revealed they were very pleased with the level and quality of service they received. Several ranked it higher than private sector employment agencies. They attributed the program's success to a highly dedicated and professional staff, the job club approach which they felt restored their self-confidence, and the Resource Center. The positive appraisal given by participants was also forthcoming from program administrators. One TEC trainer called it "the most successful jobs program I have been involved with in 18 years with TEC."

Overall, 628 of the 855 participants were placed in employment (see table 8-4) for an overall placement rate of 73.5 percent. This performance is fairly impressive given the general condition of the labor market. The cost per placement, calculated by dividing the total project allocation by the number of participants placed in unsubsidized jobs, is $1,735.

The average wage at entry for 815 participants for whom information was available was $12.78 per hour. The average wage of those placed was $9.05 per hour, for a wage replacement rate of 71 percent.

Table 8-4
Enrollment and Participation Characteristics
from October 1983 to October 1984

Selected characteristics	Transition year terminations	Percent
Total participants	855	100.0
Total terminations		
Entered employment	628	73.5
Sex		
Male	690	80.7
Female	165	19.3
Age		
14–15	0	0
16–19	0	0
20–21	4	0.5
22–44	667	78.0
45–54	112	13.1
55 and over	72	8.4
Education		
School dropout	39	4.6
Student (H.S. or less)	0	0
High school graduate or more	598	69.9
College graduate	218	25.5
Race		
White	316	37.0
Black	343	40.1
Hispanic	104	12.0
Native American	0	0
Asian	93	10.9
Employment barriers		
Limited English	2	0.2
Handicapped	12	1.4
Offender	0	0
Other	0	0
Benefit recipiency		
U.I. claimant	602	70.4
U.I. exhaustee	253	29.6
Public assistance (GA)	NA	NA
AFDC	NA	NA
Youth AFDC	NA	NA
Labor force status (prior 26 weeks)		
Unemployed 1–14 weeks	254	29.7
Unemployed 15 or more weeks	601	70.3
Not in labor force	0	0

SOURCE: JTPA Monthly Participant Status Report (completed 12/10/84).

Some of the reasons why this project had a high placement rate in spite of the fact that it was slow getting started, due to procedural problems at both the state and local level, were:

(1) the combination of HCC and TEC—agencies with long histories of working together on federal and state funded employment and training programs. Many of the high-level administrators, project managers, and training personnel at both institutions have known each other for a long time. In addition, the agencies' previous experience with externally funded programs actually enabled the project to start up faster than other Title III projects in the state because TEC was willing to proceed on the basis of a notification letter on the good faith that the funds would arrive. TEC "front-ended" the costs for three months;

(2) good "readings" of the industries to be targeted, the occupations in demand, and the characteristics of the likely participants. This was the result of fairly extensive market analyses at both the state and local level;

(3) the uniquesness of the Title III project in the Houston employment and training market; as the participant characteristics showed, a significant proportion of them were in their early forties and there was really no one particularly interested in providing the level of job search assistance and retraining that they needed to reenter employment without suffering a tremendous drop in income;

(4) a highly professional job search program mixing motivational and skill building activities on both an individual and group basis. The participant's initial contact with program personnel was in "classy" surroundings. Both the Career Circles, Inc., and TEC Job Search Assistance programs were conducted in professional office settings which was certainly different from what most of the participants expected from a "federal program." The quality of the training personnel was also outstanding in comparison with other federal programs observed. The Resource

Center was another positive factor, particularly since it gave participants a temporary office to work from in their job search efforts. Realistic counseling was another positive factor;

(5)   another factor was the flexibility provided within a somewhat fixed service sequence; participants were given flexibility in terms of time spent in various activities (specifically job search, classroom training and OJT). There was also flexibility in the training packages put together; they were tailored to each individual's skills, interests, and needs.

Some problems surfaced during the transition year. Some were externally imposed; others were not. The major problems were:

(1)   the delay in state approval of the contract; while the TEC portion of the project (job search assistance) could begin without money in hand, the HCC portion could not. The delay was one of the reasons the initial plan to combine classroom training with a job with a private employer had to be abandoned. (The other reason was the employer's market described earlier;)

(2)   the initial quasi-formal plan for serving nearly equal numbers of white-collar workers, while met, was largely a result of luck. Until the unexpected closing of the Weingarten's Grocery chain and Bama Foods, few blue-collar workers were entering the program;

(3)   getting professional and managerial white-collar workers to go through classroom training with a serious, positive attitude. A related problem was that some of these participants felt the HCC programs were too drawn out and aimed at "less intelligent" individuals. Obviously, it was originally expected that the bulk of the white-collar workers would find employment following job search assistance, while a large proportion of the blue-collar workers would need more extensive training or retraining. The most successful strategy used with white-collar professionals was to convince them to go into sales in fields related to their previous occupation;

(4)   finding OJT contractors; the nature of the local market meant that employers did not need to rely upon TEC to find workers;

(5)   for the same reason there were some difficulties experienced in generating involvement of the private sector.

Overall Assessment

Overall, this project would have to be judged a fairly successful one for the reasons cited throughout the report:

(1)   accurate and appropriate targeting of problem industries;

(2)   good gauging of characteristics of potential participants;

(3)   the design of the job search assistance portion of the project;

(4)   individualized counseling and intensive placement efforts;

(5)   high placement rates; and

(6)   low per placement costs.

In a sense, the effective overall thrust of the project was to teach participants how to repackage their skills in a format more saleable to other sectors of the local job market. There was little substantive new training, retraining, or relocation.

9
The ASARCO Copper Smelter Project

Introduction

In June of 1984, management of the ASARCO Copper Smelter in Tacoma, Washington announced the elimination of all smelting activities at that location. This announcement immediately imperiled over 600 jobs. Officials of the State of Washington, as well as Pierce and Tacoma County officials, immediately began planning what would ultimately become a request for funding for a Dislocated Worker Project from the Department of Labor's discretionary Title III funds.

For a number of reasons, the ASARCO project is a classic case for the Dislocated Worker Program. The first is the nature of the industry, because copper smelting is a declining industry in the United States. The second is the location of the industry in an urban setting. The third is the fact that the employees had been at the plant for over 15 years and were relatively well-paid. This case study examines how the project was implemented, identifies the activities provided by the project for advancing the employability of the laid off workers, and summarizes the subsequent early outcomes of the project.

The Local Labor Market

The ASARCO copper refining plant is located on the outskirts of Tacoma, Washington. The City of Tacoma and Pierce County which surrounds it operate a consortium Service Delivery Area (SDA). The city and the county are located on the south central segment of Puget

Sound. This local labor market has historically encountered more unemployment than the other major local labor market in the area— Seattle, Washington. Pierce County (Tacoma) and King County (Seattle) to the north, are connected by a relatively efficient freeway system that allows labor force mobility between the two. Therefore, the Seattle labor market must be taken into account in any examination of labor market trends within the Tacoma/Pierce County SDA.

Despite the proximity to the King County labor market, Pierce County exhibits higher unemployment rates and significantly lower per capita incomes. This is also true when comparing the Pierce County labor market to other labor markets in the State of Washington. As of July 1985, the unemployment rate in the Seattle area (King and Snohomish counties) was 6.5 percent. Across the state, Spokane, Washington was experiencing a 7.3 percent unemployment rate. The Tacoma area, however, had an unemployment rate of 8.4 percent.

Twelve percent of the state's population resides within the Pierce County labor market, however, 28 percent of the state's black population and 15 percent of the state's Asian population reside there. The population growth in the Tacoma area has been above average for the past four years. Between 1980 and 1984, the Tacoma area's population increased 6 percent. During that same time period, total employment increased at slightly over 1 percent per year. The slow growth in employment within the area was due to the severe recession of the early 1980s. Between the years of 1983 and 1984, nonagricultural employment in the Tacoma area grew by only 3.7 percent. It is uncertain whether the area has the industrial base to maintain employment growth equal to expected population changes.

The higher rates of unemployment are reflected in the relative income level of the area. In 1983, the average per capita income for the State of Washington was $12,427. In the King County labor market, average per capita income was $14,577. However, Pierce County's per capita income was $11,010, or 11 percent less than the urban average and one-fourth less than the average for the neighboring labor market to the north, King County. That 30,000 military personnel reside in Pierce County explains only part of the income differential.

Table 9-1 below indicates the employment mix in the Tacoma/Pierce County labor market. In 1984, 6,000 workers were employed by the area's lumber and paper products industries. This represents 4 percent of the total wage and salary employment in the area. During that same year, those two industries represented 10 percent of the total insured unemployed in the Tacoma/Pierce County labor market. Employment in the lumber industry is down almost 28 percent from its peak in 1978-79.

Several other key industries within the area have suffered significant employment setbacks in the 1980s. The area's boat building and aluminum industries have recently experienced declines in employment. For instance, Tacoma Boat, the major boat builder in the area, at one time employed over 3,000 workers; there are now fewer than 800 employees.

The long-run effect of these changes on the Tacoma area is unclear. While ASARCO has closed and Tacoma Boat and the lumber industries are suffering, the city has experienced large additions to employment at the Tacoma Port and employment is growing in the hotel industry and in other selected industries, e.g., Fairchild Camera and Equipment.

In summary, the Tacoma/Pierce County labor market is currently experiencing relatively high rates of unemployment. Per capita income within this labor market is lower than the average for the State of Washington. The differences are even more apparent when comparing Tacoma/Pierce County with the area directly to the north. A significant proportion of the area's employment problems are long term and structural. Tacoma's past dependence on employment in industries such as lumber, pulp and paper, and boat building have produced a core of unemployed that require extensive training in order to become employable.

State Organizationof Title III

The State of Washington's Employment Security Department administers the Title III program. Within the Employment Security Depart-

Table 9-1
Nonagricultural Wage and Salary Workers Employed in the Tacoma Metropolitan Area, Pierce County
(In thousands)

	June 1984[1]	May 1984	June 1983	Change	
				May 1984-June 1984	June 1983-June 1984
Total[2]	146.7	147.1	145.4	− 0.4	+ 1.3
Total manufacturing	20.6	20.6	21.1	0	− 0.5
Food and kindred products	2.4	2.3	2.4	+ 0.1	0
Lumber and wood products	4.5	4.3[4]	4.4	+ 0.2	+ 0.1
Furniture and fixtures	0.6	0.6	0.6	0	0
Paper and allied products	1.5	1.5	1.5	0	0
Chemicals and allied products	0.8	0.7	0.8	+ 0.1	0
Primary metals	1.5	1.5	1.5	0	0
Fabricated metal products & machinery (excl. electrical)	1.4	1.5	1.9	− 0.1	− 0.5
Transportation equipment	2.4	2.9	3.4	− 0.5	− 1.0
All other manufacturing[3]	5.5	5.3	4.6	+ 0.2	+ 0.9
Construction	7.1	6.8	6.5	+ 0.3	+ 0.6
Transportation and public utilities	7.1	7.2	7.0	− 0.1	+ 0.1
Wholesale and retail trade	36.8	36.7	35.9	+ 0.1	+ 0.9
Finance, insurance and real estate	7.2	7.2	7.2	0	0
Services and mining	33.6	34.3	32.9	− 0.7	+ 0.7
Government	34.3	34.3	34.8	0	− 0.5

1. Preliminary.
2. Excludes proprietors, self-employed, members of armed services, workers in private households, and agricultural workers. Includes all full- and part-time wage and salary workers receiving pay during the pay period including the 12th of the month.
3. Includes apparel; printing and publishing; stone, clay, and glass; and miscellaneous manufacturing.
4. Employment affected by labor-management disputes.

ment, the Training Program Services Division actually implements Title III activities and is also responsible for the statewide JTPA program (see figure 9-1). Within the Training Program Services Division, the Title III program is under the control of the deputy assistant commissioner. In addition to Title III, the deputy assistant commissioner also manages the state council staff as well as the state's Title IIA set asides. The Title III program director reports to this deputy assistant commissioner. The organization chart which follows identifies the relationship between the director of the state's Title III program and the commissioner of Employment Security. The actual implementation of Title III activities is thus relatively far removed from the commissioner's office and correspondingly the governor's office.

The formula-funded Title III funds are allocated through two mechanisms. The first is titled Special Employment Training Services (SETS), which operates in 23 of the Job Service centers throughout the state. In theory, reemployment services are targeted to the general dislocated worker population, that is, those not associated with large plant closures. The SETS funds were allocated to the 23 Job Service centers throughout the state by a formula that incorporated size of the civilian labor force, the number of unemployed individuals, the number of unemployed insurance exhaustees, and the number of excess unemployed, or the number of unemployed in excess of 4.5 percent of the civilian labor force, in the relevant area. SETS services include skills assessment, job search workshops, institutional skills training, OJT, relocation, and placement assistance. Most participants are unemployment insurance claimants who face barriers to reemployment because of technological or industrial change. Historically, SETS has accounted for over 50 percent of all Title III funds in the State of Washington. Program year 1984 funding for Title III formula funds amounted to approximately $3,819,532 of which the SETS accounted for $1,685,744.

The second approach is plant- or industry-specific projects that provide services to specific groups of workers affected by closures or mass layoffs. Typically, projects are identified by the state staff and then im-

Figure 9-1
Washington State Employment Security Department

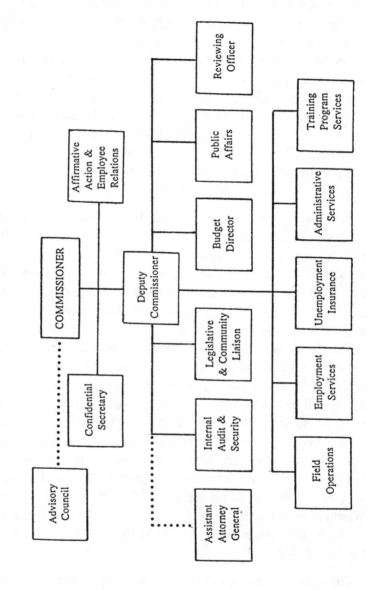

plemented through cooperation with local Employment Security, company, union, and locally elected officials.

The state guidelines for defining a dislocated worker are as follows:

(1) the individual has been terminated or received notice of termination from employment;

(2) the individual is eligible for or has exhausted entitlement to unemployment compensation; and

(3) the individual is unlikely to return to employment in the individual's principal occupation or previous industry because of the diminishing demand for their skills in that occupation or industry.

As of November 1985, the State of Washington had four projects operating from the regular Title III obligation funding, and an additional four projects operating or about to operate with discretionary funds allocated by the Secretary of Labor.

The ASARCO Resource Center operates the project for the Employment Security Department. In actuality, the Resource Center is an appendage of the Tacoma Employment Security Job Service Center. The Center's director reports to the director of the Tacoma Employment Security who then reports to the Field Operations Division of the Employment Security Department. The Field Operations Division is the entity that has been granted the funding for Title III activities by the Training Program Services Division within the Employment Security Department. Thus, all Title III projects in the state, whether they operate under the SETS format, the project format, or whether they are projects that are being funded by the Secretary's discretionary funds, are all supervised and to some extent actually implemented by Employment Security personnel.

In general, there were no specific requirements for targeting Title III funding to a particular firm, industry, geographic area, or occupation. However, the state has allocated Title III funds to a specific area in the state where there are many dislocated workers in the wood products and fishing industries. A special task force and a significant amount of funds were assigned a five-county area in southwest Washington where these industries are predominantly located.

In summary, the governor's office, through the Employment Security Department, controls the funding for Title III within the state. The Employment Security Department operates the SETS program through its 23 centers throughout the state and is responsible for initiating and administering the various Title III projects. While local government officials, SDA officials, union officials, and private sector individuals are involved in an advisory capacity, it is clear that the state has decided to use a centrally controlled implementation model for funding all of the Title III activities.

Nature of the Project

The closing of the ASARCO copper smelter resulted from a world copper glut which significantly decreased the market price for refined copper. This, in combination with the expected future cost increases for continued production at the ASARCO plant, forced company officials to discontinue operation at their Tacoma facility.

State and local Employment Security officials immediately initiated a plan for Title III funding. The response was so immediate because the closure of the ASARCO plant was highly visible and represented one of the 10 largest employers in the Tacoma area. In addition, state officials were confident that they could provide a full array of training possibilities to the unemployed workers because of the location of the plant. In the past, state officials had been involved in several Title III projects located in rural areas. Not only were there few alternative occupations in these rural areas, but the training facilities available were extremely limited. The closure of the ASARCO plant allowed state and local Employment Security officials to develop a traditional Dislocated Worker Project in an urban area. The need for such a project was obvious and the state was confident federal funding could be obtained.

The state decided to fund the ASARCO project by requesting Secretary's discretionary funds. This was done because of the timing of the project; all of the formula Title III funds had been obligated. At the time of the ASARCO proposal to the Department of Labor, the state had obligated their formula Title III funds in the following manner:

Special Employment & Training Services (SETS)	$1,685,744
Research & Analysis (Special Title III Reports)	10,000
Aerospace Modification through December 1984	169,821
Office of Dislocated Worker Administration	561,494
Task Force on Reemployment Set Aside	1,112,473
Washington Tree Project	250,000
ASARCO	30,000
Totals	$3,819,532

It is possible that setting aside 46 percent of the total Title III funds for one program (SETS) reduced the state's ability to use formula funding for the ASARCO project. State officials also indicated in their proposal that there were no other federal or state resources available to help the ASARCO workers. They noted that the ASARCO worker's pay scale probably placed them in an income category that would make them ineligible for JTPA Title IIA.

The shutdown of the ASARCO plant ultimately resulted in 600 people losing their jobs. The objective of the project was to retrain 300 of those individuals to the point that they could find other occupational opportunities within the Tacoma area. The original proposal to the Secretary of Labor requested $591,355 for this purpose. Later, more monies were made available to the project through the Secretary of Labor's Copper and Steel Workers Fund. This amounted to an additional $400,000.

The Employment Security Department, through its Tacoma Job Service Center, set up a resource center on-site at the ASARCO plant. The ASARCO Resource Center developed a project that basically had four components. The first activities were entitled "pre-layoff assistance programs." These activities included information gathering, scheduling workshops and meetings with employees to familiarize them with the program, contacting potential training institutions and employers, assisting clients with resume preparation, and developing workshops on "transferrable skills identification," i.e., trying to demonstrate to the workers that they can do something other than make copper. The other three components of the project—actual job search and relocation assistance, job training, and finally job development and placement—became integral parts of the ASARCO Resource Center as the plant actually started its shutdown phase in March 1985.

The announcement by ASARCO of its intention to close its plant almost a year before the actual shutdown date allowed state officials to initiate relatively thorough preproject implementation research. For instance, the ASARCO Resource Center staff was able to assemble a local task force, identify and initiate an employee survey, formally announce the program to the employees, canvass the area for services, resources, and labor market information, develop plans and funding proposals for additional resources, identify sources of matching funds, plan the actual sequence of services for each worker, and determine actual needs for clients while they were still working at the plant. By the time of the actual shutdown in the spring of 1985, Employment Security officials were aware of the demographic characteristics of the population they were going to serve, had identified over a score of classroom training activities within the area that would be appropriate for the workers, and had determined their clients' needs and future expectations.

The Advisory Task Force set up by the ASARCO Resource Center included political (local, state and federal) officials, Employment Security (local and state) officials, one ASARCO official (the personnel officer), four union members, two United Way representatives, the local SDA director, who served as chairman of the group, and two members of Tacoma's Economic Development Board. Note that this group did not include any private sector representatives other than from ASARCO, nor did it include any training institution representatives. The task force provided the resource center with the input in the initial stages of the project. However, the absence of private sector involvement may be felt toward the end of the project when the Center is primarily engaged in placement activities. Normally, private sector involvement is an effective way of advertising the existence of the project to employers within the labor market.

Union involvement in this project has been extensive. Of the 17 members of the Advisory Task Force, four represent the labor union, specifically the two labor unions involved in the plant shutdown, as well as representation by the state labor organization. Further, the union donated its building to the ASARCO Resource Center and was involved in communicating details of the project to the workers while the plant was still operating. With the help of the unions involved, the ASARCO Resource Center was able to contact over 450 of the ASARCO workers by January of 1985.

Obviously, the unions were involved in the negotiations over severance pay for the ASARCO workers. The eventual agreement allowed each union member a $50 per week supplementary unemployment benefit for up to one year after layoff. In addition, after one year, each worker receives severance pay. The amount of the severance pay depends upon the worker's years of seniority. The minimum amount of severance is for two years seniority and is $896.00. The maximum amount of severance pay is for an individual with 15 or more years and is $13,700. One hundred and eighteen union members took early retirement and were granted severance pay of from $9,780 to $14,900. In addition, these individuals will receive a $300 a month pension until the age of 62. They will then be eligible for their normal retirement benefits.

In summary, the ASARCO Title III project was implemented in response to the plant closing by state and local officials. It was designed and implemented with Title III formula and discretionary funds, special funds for copper and steel industries made available by the Department of Labor, and Trade Readjustment Funds. Given the advance notice, it did not face the time constraints experienced by many Title III projects. The ASARCO Advisory Task Force included a wide range of public sector representatives and union officials, but lacked a representative sampling from the private sector. Finally, there was significant union involvement in the project.

Project Design and Services

The ASARCO Resource Center implemented the project in three phases. The first phase, which started in late summer 1984, involved outreach and enrollment. The Resource Center attempted to notify all 600 eligible workers and engaged in general advertising while the plant was still operational. Initial activities included getting all of the workers to complete applications, providing all applicants orientation to the program, counseling applicants on the necessity of setting realistic goals and objectives, referring clients to other available community resources, scheduling and conducting skill profile assessments, familiarizing the applicants with the Washington Occupational Information System, referring and enrolling clients in vocational training, coordinating with the local United Way to conduct preretirement workshops, and developing community programs for information on self-employment.

The second phase of activities within the ASARCO Resource Center, initiated generally in the spring of 1985, included job search workshops. These workshops included the following: acquiring sources for job search, identifying and matching the individual's job skills to job openings, accessing the hidden job market, developing self-confidence, resume writing and effective job interview skills, identifying the enrollment procedures in vocational training institutes, and developing short vocational school courses for brushing up existing skills that might enable individuals to get into the job market quickly.

The final phase of Resource Center activities is generating placements for their clients. This phase was started approximately in mid-summer 1985 and is on-going. The components within this phase include: searching local, state and national job openings as listed by the Job Service Centers, interviewing employers in order to develop employer/client relationships, researching newspaper want ads, providing resources for job search for the clients, i.e., access to phones for local and long distance calls, adding additional support services, e.g., tools, travel pay and clothing, providing space for interviewing by recruiters, and, finally, classes and short programs to provide motivation and encouragement for participants. Two other components of this phase included developing OJT contracts with employers in the local area, and providing relocation assistance to clients who found jobs outside of the local area.

Of the 364 clients enrolled by the ASARCO Resource Center, 221 individuals were involved in classroom training programs. The project included 30 on-the-job training contracts. The remaining clients of the ASARCO Resource Center were enrolled in workshops on job-finding skills as well as in the group- and self-directed job search programs.

Over 100 institutional training programs were funded by the Resource Center (see table 9-2). The vast majority of all the classroom training courses were year-long vocational courses and the majority were for one to three clients. One exception was the real estate training which was only a six-week activity. Three programs were relatively large, one (refrigeration mechanics) had 19 participants, another (computer repair) had 32 participants, and a truck driving program had 12 participants.

The administrators preferred the longer term training because they believed there was a greater likelihood of longer term placement. The costs of these programs varied from $60 a client to nearly $3,000 per client. The overall average was $1,500–$1,700 per training activity per participant.

As of April 30, 1987, the project had spent approximately $1,300 per participant for institutional training, needs-based payments, on-the-job training, post-support services, relocation and support services.

The classroom training offered by the ASARCO project was more diversified, required more skill, and lasted longer on the average than the typical array of classroom training programs offered in the area under Title IIA. This reflected the fact that these dislocated workers were higher skilled than the Title IIA participants. However, in most cases, they were so specialized that their skills had to be augmented, even if there were jobs available in their occupation. Copper smelting produced ex-

Table 9-2
Institutional Training Programs for ASARCO Workers

Asbestos Removal	Auto Mechanic
Auto Trimmer, Glazier	Appliance Repairer
Auto Service Center Specialist	Accounting for Comptrollers
Automotive Manager	Auto Body Mechanic
Accountant/Bookkeeper	Automotive Repair
Building Design Technician	Bookkeeper
Boiler Operator	Broadcast Technician
Building Maintenance	Brick Mason
Computer Repair Preparation	Custodial Engineer
Computer Repair Technician	Cost Engineering
Computer Field Technician	Corrections Officer
Consumer Electronics Technician	Computer Repair Technician
Commercial Truckdriving	CNC Machining
Commercial Painter	Computer Programming
Civil Engineering Technician	Crane Operator
Concrete Technologist	CVC Mach., Intro
Computer Keyboard	Computer Technician
Community Photographer	Carpenter, Mfd. Buildings
Computer Service & Representative	Digital Electronic Technician
Diesel Mechanics	D/S Reprographics
Electronic Technician Certification	Small Engine Repair
Electronic Security Technician	Environmental Science
Small Engine Mechanic	Electronic Equipment Service Technician
Entrepreneur	Electronic Equipment Technician
Electrical Engineer	Electronics Technician
Electronics Appliance Technician	Carpet Installer
Food Service Specialist	Food Processor Machine Mechanic
Farrier	First Aid
Financial Paraprofessional Planner	Food Processor, Machine Repair
Food Mixer Repairer	Greenhouse Worker
Graphic Artist	Heating Mechanic Helper
Hydraulics/Electric	Heating & Air Mechanic
Industrial Repair	Inside/Outside Sales
Inventory Clerk	Millwright
Industrial Fluid Power	Jeweler
Landscape/Turf Management	Landscape Gardener
Maintenance Mechanic	Management Nursery/Greenhouse
Motorcycle Mechanic	Mobile Elec. Comm. Technician
Maintenance Repairer	Marine Mechanic
Manufactured Housing Technician	Math & Reading Lab
NC/CNC Machining	Marine Diesel Mechanic
Machinery Mechanic	Machinist Helper
Mechanic Heavy Equipment	Office Machine Mechanic
Parts Merchandiser	Purchasing Agent
Refrigeration & Air Condition	Refrigeration & Air Condition Mechanic
Refrigeration & Air Condition Technician	Refrigeration Mechanic

Table 9-2 (continued)

R.V. Mechanic	R.V. Repair
Real Estate Agent	Refrigeration Technician
Route Sales & Repair	Small Business Management
Sheet Metal Apprentice	Security Officer
Security Equipment	Warehouse/Sales
Sheet Metal Worker	Sheet Metal Mechanic
Service Station Manager	Stationary Engineer
Television Broadcast	Transportation Traffic Technician
Truckdriver	Terminal Operator
Telephone Equip. Repair & Installation	Tool Programmer
Transportation Traffic Technician	Television Broadcast Technician
Truck Trailer Mechanic	Truck Trailer Mechanic
Vending Machine Mechanic	Vending Machine Repair
Welder Pipe	Welding Inspector I
Wastewater Treatment Operator	Warehouse Shipping/Receiving
Word Processing	Water Supply Technician
Welding	Warehouse/Sales

tremely job-specific skill training. For example, officials at the Resource Center identified an industrial repairman from the ASARCO plant who had never worked with hydraulics. Supplemental training for eight weeks in hydraulics, however, landed him a job as a diesel repair specialist in another plant.

In nearly all cases, the training was in regular courses in community colleges, vocational technical institutes, or private training institutions. The training time or curriculum did not vary for participants within each training program.

The intensity of the classroom training activities seemed to be relatively high. For instance, the refrigerator mechanics program was only 12 hours per week, but these individuals commute two hours per day to go to this program. The computer repair program was 35 hours per week. The trucking program was 19 hours per week. Overall, the classroom training averaged 30 plus hours a week. The Resource Center staff believed most participants put in a relatively full workweek in training.

The ASARCO Resource Center staff screened applicants for the individual classroom training programs. Individuals who were not deemed appropriate for a specific classroom training program were redirected to another vocational area. The Resource Center spent a lot of time trying to identify the right program for the particular individual. For this reason, there was a wide range of training programs offered for the program participants (126 programs for 221 participants).

In summary, the ASARCO Resource Center has offered the normal array of activities for a Dislocated Worker Program. However, it was decided to spend a large part of the funds for relatively expensive classroom training. Over two-thirds of the clients participated in classroom training programs. The remaining one-third of the ASARCO Resource Center's clients were engaged in workshop training and job search skills. OJT and support services rounded out the array of program activities offered by the Center.

Eligible Population

The eligible population for this project was composed of the employees of the ASARCO plant as of June 1984. This represented approximately 600 workers. Employees at the plant were represented by two unions. The production workers were represented by the United Steel Workers of America, AFL-CIO, Local 25; the office and chemical laboratory employees were members of the Automotive and Special Services Union, Local 461, Teamsters Union. Approximately 78 percent of the workers in the ASARCO plant were hourly, and nearly all of the hourly workers were unionized. The hourly workers' pay averaged approximately $2,154 a month or $12.43 per hour. This was significantly above the average monthly pay for the Tacoma area of $1,412.

Table 9-3 below indicates the characteristics of the participants in the project. The group was heavily male, relatively old, generally white and relatively well-educated. There were, for example, only eight individuals with limited English-speaking ability. They represented a classic dislocated worker population. The majority had worked approximately 15 or more years at the ASARCO plant and were receiving between $25,000 and $30,000 a year.

Table 9-3
Enrollment and Participant Characteristics for the ASARCO
Dislocated Worker Project (as of 4/30/87)

	Dislocated workers
I. Participation and Termination Summary	
A. Total participants	366
B. Total terminations	306
1. Entered unsubsidized employment	260
2. All other terminations	
participating in pre-layoff assistance	1
C. Total current participants	57
D. Total transferred to other subrecipients	3
E. Average weeks at termination	55
F. Average hourly wage at termination	$9.74
II. Terminees' characteristics at program entry	
1. Male	297
2. Female	9
3. 16–21	5
4. 22–29	25
5. 30–54	249
6. 55 and over	27
7. School dropout	37
8. Student (high school or less)	—
9. High school graduate or equivalent	203
10. Post high school attendee	66
11. White	270
12. Black	23
13. Hispanic	8
14. American Indian or Alaskan Native	4
15. Asian or Pacific Islander	1
16. Single parent with dependent(s) under 18	1
17. Limited English language proficiency	6
18. Handicapped	5
19. Offender	—
20. Unemployment Compensation claimant	80
21. Exhaustees	1
22. Unemployed 15 or more weeks of prior 26	73
23. Not in labor force	225

Program Outcomes

Initially, placement of ASARCO workers was relatively slow. For instance, only 53 individuals were placed by the Resource Center by October 1, 1985. There were several rationales for this modest initial placement rate. First, since the majority of the classroom training offered was relatively long term, few participants had terminated by this time. Second, the economic environment of the Tacoma area made it hard to identify job openings. Third, the ASARCO workers were initially receiving unemployment compensation as well as layoff supplements under the union contract. These resources, as well as their future severance pay, may have affected their inclination to search for a job. The ASARCO Resource Center had initial difficulty recruiting clients for their job search workshops. The Center offered a relatively lengthy workshop (15 hours). Many clients did not sign up until their alternative resources had been exhausted and they experienced the need for employment.

The typical unemployed ASARCO worker received approximately $185 a week from unemployment compensation and an additional $50 a week in supplemental unemployment pay under the labor agreement. Thus, they were receiving roughly $940 a month tax-free while unemployed. In addition, approximately one year after layoff they received severance payments averaging $4,000 per worker. These workers had been earning from $1,550 to $1,700 in take-home pay when they were working at ASARCO. Early in the project's development an official noted that a significant segment of the ASARCO population appeared to be not actively seeking employment or participating in the retraining process at the ASARCO Resource Center. The official pointed out that the ASARCO workers had been working in an industry which had had quite a few strikes, they had experienced layoffs in the past, and they were used to long periods of unemployment. In addition, there may also have been some disaving by the unemployed ASARCO workers.

Finally, ASARCO project administrators stressed the use of intensive job-search programs and time-intensive institutional training. Approximately 220 individuals, two-thirds of all participants, were involved in institutional training. Therefore, it took the average participant a relatively long time to be prepared for actual job placement (55 weeks).

A total of 364 participants were served by the ASARCO Resource Center. More recent figures than those in table 9-3 indicate that 278 individuals were placed in unsubsidized employment. The jobs paid an average wage of over $9 per hour—near the average for all workers in the Tacoma area.

Table 9-4 indicates the range of occupations in which the ASARCO workers were placed. (Only 65 percent of the actual jobs are included in table 9-4.) It is apparent that the Resource Center placed program participants in every conceivable sector of the Tacoma labor market.

The project's original goals were all reached or exceeded. Eighty-five percent of the program terminees were placed, approximately 76 percent were placed in jobs with wages averaging 50 percent more than the national figures for Title III progrms—$6.61 an hour.

These outcomes were achieved by funding a variety of services for the participants. Costs of direct services for participants (institutional skill training, on-the-job training, and supportive services) varied dramatically (from $5 to $6,268 per participant). The average expenditure per participant approached $1,000 as of May 1, 1987. However, 10 percent of participants received direct services costing less than $100. The remaining participants received direct services costing, on average, $1,400.

Overall Assessment

There is no doubt that the ASARCO Copper Smelter project was an extremely successful program. The average placement rate of terminees was 85 percent. The project served 20 percent more people than originally targeted. While many of the participants did enter jobs that paid 30 percent less than they were receiving before the plant shutdown, they did, on the average, find jobs that paid 50 percent more than the national average for Title III programs. Further, this was accomplished

Table 9-4
Placements for ASARCO Workers

Occupational title	Est. hourly wage rate	Occupational title	Est. hourly wage rate
Repair Helper	6.00	Assembler, Installer	9.24
Truckdriver	10.80	Brick Mason	12.00
Dispatcher	5.15	Sheet Metal Worker	9.36
Laborer	17.85	Machine Feeder	7.00
Laborer	7.25	Sider	15.00
Electronics Technician	6.00	Ski Maker	5.25
Stationary Engineer	7.00	Owner	10.00
Remodeling Contractor	10.00	Heating Refrig. Air Cond.	9.50
Laborer	9.25	Painter Helper	7.00
Baggage Handler	6.00	Waste Collector	9.13
Laborer	5.29	Equipment Operator	14.00
Truckdriver, Light Truck	4.50	Warehouseman	11.60
Electronics Technician	3.65	Glass Finisher	9.50
Employment Interviewer	9.28	Assembler, Installer	9.24
Tune-up Mechanic	4.50	Rate Clerk	5.50
Electronics Technician	6.00	Steel Fitter	12.00
Carpenter/Laborer	9.00	Appliance Repair Technician	8.00
Industrial Repair	13.37	Die Casting Mach. Helper	8.00
Building Maintenance	6.83	Baker/Owner	10.00
Pipe Fitter	12.00	Truckdriver	9.90
Box Maker	4.00	Licensed Nurse	5.49
Custodian	7.40	Security Officer	5.75
Industrial Painter	12.00	Truckdriver	14.53
Farrier	10.00	Maintenance Mechanic	13.00
Landscape Lawn Service	9.75	RV Mechanic	8.00
Records Clerk	10.75	Truckdriver	10.80
Security Equipment	9.00	Material Handler	7.00
Industrial Repairer	12.75	Bus Driver	4.50
Pipe Layer Helper	8.00	Painter Helper	10.37
Die Casting Mach. Helper	7.60	Crane Operator	10.00
Beekeeper	7.00	Inventory Clerk	10.04
Truckdriver	14.00	Installer	7.00
Pipe Fitter Helper	6.00	Brick Mason	12.00
Brick Mason	13.00	Security Guard	4.50
Surveyor Helper	7.00	Landscaper Gardener	5.00
Glazier	8.53	Custodian	5.49
Laborer, Salvage	8.45	Landscaper	4.50
Laborer, General	4.00	Jeweler	5.00
Service Station Manager	4.50	Warehouse Worker	5.00
Crane Operator	13.35	Electronics Technician	8.07
Maintenance Mechanic	11.00	Electrician	11.62
Material Handler	8.00	Data Entry Operator	6.75
Technician, TV	10.70	Industrial Repairman	12.75

although the program included participants who were very difficult to place (truly structurally unemployed) in an area with a relatively high unemployment rate.

The evidence points to six factors that account for the project's favorable performance. State officials point out that the early notification of plant closure allowed time for planning by employment and training staff, as well as offering the workers time to prepare for the required career adjustment. Second, because only one plant was involved, the program focused on a relatively homogeneous group of workers. This, in turn, produced a group of participants who were close knit and extremely receptive toward the program offered by the ASARCO Resource Center.

While early notification and cooperation between program staff and participants obviously enhanced the program, other factors may have had a larger effect on the program's final performance. Specifically these are:

the project focused on institutional skill training;

the project received funding from a variety of sources that allowed for considerable flexibility in the services offered;

the project lasted for over two and one-half years; and

the project was well funded.

A General Accounting Office report noted that nationally, fewer than one-half of Title III program participants received occupational skill training. In addition, fewer than one-fourth received support services.[1] The ASARCO Resource Center, however, funded occupational skill training for over 60 percent of its participants. (They also funded on-the-job training for an additional 10 percent of program participants.) One-half of the program participants received support services (including relocation and needs-based payments).

The availability of Trade Adjustment Act funds in addition to formula and discretionary Title III funds meant that support services were generously funded. As of April 30, 1987, the ASARCO Center had spent $216,353 directly on institutional skill training. An additional $50,263 had been spent on "on-the-job training." Other support in terms of needs-based payments, supportive services, and general support services accounted for an additional $77,988 or 23 percent of total program expenditures. The amount of resources as well as the flexibility in their use (for example, at least two individuals received over $2,000 each in tools and equipment) allowed program administrators to place clients in quality institutional skill training programs.

Training and placing dislocated workers is a complex and time-consuming task. The ASARCO Resource Center was funded for over two and one-half years. This allowed the staff to develop individualized training programs that were not constrained by short-term time horizons. It also allowed sufficient time for outreach, for intensive training, and, finally, for job search activities. Thus, the ASARCO Resource Center's staff were able to perform an admirable job in placing their clients.

Obviously, skill training, funding for support services, and the project's length were all directly related to the total funding available for the project. The ASARCO Resource Center had $1,046,000 allocated directly to the project, and an additional $800,000 in matching funds. This allowed project administrators to fund skill training, to provide adequate support services, and, in the end, to place 76 percent of those participants who lost their jobs as a result of the ASARCO plant closure.

NOTE

1. U.S. General Accounting Office, *Dislocated Workers: Local Programs and Outcomes Under the Job Training Partnership Act*, GAO/HRD-87-41, Washington, D.C., March 1987, table 4.1, p. 46.

10
The Dane County, Wisconsin Dislocated Worker Project

Introduction

Dane County, Wisconsin, which includes the City of Madison, has a heavily white-collar labor force with unemployment concentrated among blue-collar workers in the manufacturing and construction industries. This project, operated by a consortium of three community-based organizations, was designed for Title III eligibles in the county, with priority given to former employees of Giddings and Lewis, a foundry that closed.

The Nature of the Labor Market

The local labor market is generally considered to be Dane County, with its population of 323,545 and labor force of about 185,000. Unemployment is persistently low in this labor market, in which one-third of all workers are employed by government or the University of Wisconsin. The current unemployment rate of 4.8 percent, however, conceals the much higher rates in construction and manufacturing. About 20 percent of workers in Dane County belong to unions, with about 20 percent craft unions, 40 percent industrial and service unions, and 40 percent public employee unions. Real growth in new jobs in Dane County in recent years (see table 10-1) has not been in the public sector, but in service and trade jobs, as well as in the financial, real estate, and insurance industries. High-paying jobs associated with the construction and manufacturing industries are becoming an endangered species.

Table 10-1
Dane County, Wisconsin
Workforce Distribution and Percent Change from 1978 to 1983

Sector	1978	Percent of workforce	1983	Percent of workforce	Percent change
Transportation & public utilities	5,400	3.5	6,300	3.6	+16.6
Contract construction	7,400	4.7	5,400	3.0	−27.0
Finance, real estate, insurance	11,300	7.2	13,300	7.6	+17.7
Manufacturing	17,800	11.4	19,000	10.8	+6.7
Services	25,800	16.5	35,000	19.9	+35.7
Trade	35,500	22.8	40,100	22.8	+13.0
Government	52,700	33.8	56,400	32.1	+7.0
Total	155,900		175,600		+12.6

NOTE: The construction figure reflects the lingering recession in that industry. Manufacturing, while showing an increase shows that increase primarily in skilled and semi-skilled jobs.

Employment in Dane County, already very white and very white-collar, is becoming more so. The few major manufacturing firms are cutting back or closing all together.

A letter of support for the proposal for this project by the president of the Madison Federation of Labor notes:

> For example, in the last two years, production employment at the Oscar Mayer plant has dropped from 2,000 to 1,500 (on top of a reduction of well over 1,000 in previous years). Production worker employment at Dairy Equipment has dropped from 440 to 90 in the last two years. According to the union representatives of these workers, most of those who have been laid off in the past year have not been able to find new jobs.
>
> Giddings & Lewis announced a couple of weeks ago that it intends to close (permanently) its foundry in Madison. That foundry currently employs 45 workers; their average seniority is 20 years. Another 60 workers are currently on lay-off status; an additional 30 or so have just recently lost recall rights. Nearly all of these workers and the ones mentioned above desperately need re-training, counseling, and placement aid.[1]

This shift away from blue-collar employment is reflected in the list below, submitted as part of the Title III application:

Expanding
Chemical & Allied
Finance, Real Estate
  and Insurance
Trade, Retail Services
Scientific & Control
  Instruments

Steady
Agriculture
Transportation, Communications
  and Utilities
Printing and Publishing
Food and Kindred Products
Rubber & Plastics

Recovering
Non-Electrical Machinery
Construction
Stone, Clay, Glass
Primary Metals

Weak
All Government
Fabricated Metals
Electrical & Electronics
  Machinery

In a labor market study commissioned by the Greater Madison Task Force for Planning Occupational Skills Education, labor analysts prepared table 10-2, estimating annual average job openings by occupation, from both growth and turnover. The conclusion is that between 1980 and 1990, the largest number of job openings will be in four categories: clerical; professional, technical and kindred; service; and managers and officials. Operators and laborers show a net loss in jobs.

A local survey done by the voc-tech school showed popular support here for the retention and expansion of blue-collar jobs. The city's three-year economic development plan emphasizes (on paper) the importance of expanding private sector production, especially in those sectors in which the country is importing goods from basic industries which operate elsewhere. Yet, as reflected in the statistics presented, the shift away from blue-collar employment continues.

When the shutdown of the Giddings and Lewis foundry was announced, the president of the labor federation, in consultation with the local steelworkers union at the plant, got funding for a feasibility study of whether the plant was economically viable. The study concluded that while the foundry was not state of the art, its problems resulted mainly from an absence of any attempt to find additional markets. It had been used by its conglomerate owner as an in-house foundry, part of a vertical integration, and now that the owner needed the capacity of only one of its two foundries, it was shutting down the Madison operation. Production at the Madison plant was of good quality and at reasonable cost.

As a result of the study, Wisconsin Community Development Finance Authority staff and union representatives wanted to explore keeping the foundry open. They felt that Madison elected officials were noticeably passive, first in helping to explore the possibility of keeping the foundry open, and second, in conducting the negotiations necessary to allow local economic development people to even attempt to find a buyer and develop a market.

Table 10-2
Estimated Annual Average Job Openings for Dane County, 1980 through 1990

Occupation	Mechanical projections			Judgmental projections		
	Total	Growth	Separations	Total	Growth	Separations
Personal service workers	117	46	71	0	0	0
Sales workers	640	198	441	452	140	312
Health service workers	235	100	135	110	47	63
Food service workers	751	251	500	537	179	358
Protective service workers	448	139	309	448	139	309
Service workers – all	1,954	641	1,313	1,954	641	1,313
Profession, technical & kindred occupations	1,445	551	894	2,340	893	1,447
Clerical – office machine operatives	73	26	47	50	18	32
Clerical – secretarial, steno & typists	356	122	234	439	150	289
Clerical – all positions	2,224	547	1,677	2,224	547	1,677
Clerical – other clerical workers	1,235	395	840	385	123	262
Managers and officials	1,018	293	725	1,596	460	1,136
Cleaning service workers	300	70	230	487	114	373
Transportation equipment operatives	233	80	153	163	56	107
Crafts and kindred occupations	720	233	497	504	156	348
Other service workers	67	29	38	53	23	30
Operatives, except transportation	418	120	298	- 184		
Laborers, except farm	454	128	326	- 116		
All other operatives	78	20	58	- 36		

State Organization of Title III

This project operated during the period March 5, 1984 through December 31, 1984. While it was funded by both transition year 1984 and program year 1984 Title III funds, the project was selected during the transition year 1984 funding process. Therefore, this report will discuss the Title III administrative arrangements and processes which were in effect at that time.

At the time this project was funded, the Governor's Employment and Training Office (GETO) was responsible for the administration of JTPA. The agency had been created by an executive order in 1975 in a reorganization of the CETA administrative structure. In January 1983, approximately two weeks after the new democratic governor was inaugurated, he signed an executive order continuing the Governor's Employment and Training Office and giving the agency responsibility for the funding decisions and administration of JTPA.

GETO was given cabinet level status in that executive order. Previously, most administrative functions, i.e., payroll, personnel and data processing, had been handled by the Department of Industry, Labor, and Human Relations (DILHR). As of January 31, 1983, all administrative functions were taken in-house.

At the time this project was selected, the director of GETO was appointed by, and served at the pleasure of, the governor. The director reported to the governor and attended all cabinet meetings with him to brief him on employment and training issues.

Subsequently, there has been a major restructuring in the administration of the JTPA program in the State of Wisconsin. Responsibility for JTPA has been transferred to the Department of Industry, Labor and Human Relations and, pending legislative approval, as of July 1, 1985 GETO will become a division there. As part of DILHR, the Wisconsin Title III JTPA program will have direct access to the governor through the cabinet position of the DILHR department head and through the division administrator. The present executive director of GETO will become the division administrator within DILHR.

The allocation procedures for Title III in Wisconsin have changed over time. Initially, with eligibility broadly defined, allowable program services all inclusive, and a program purpose statement which was very general, the Title III monies were amenable to political distribution. About 85 percent of the fiscal year 1983 and transition year 1984 monies were allocated without an RFP.

The remaining transition year 1984 funds were distributed through two rounds of competitive funding (RFP) and through a reserve fund ($170,000 transition year 1984, $400,000 program year 1984) through which the state could respond quickly to plant closings or assist new industry or employers. The latter was considered an open RFP.

By the time of the second round of RFPs, under which the Dane County project was funded, the program was operating under the following program purpose/intent:

> To develop and implement projects under the Wisconsin Re-employment Program that will assist dislocated workers and their families in overcoming the obstacles of unemployment and help facilitate workers' reentry into the work force at their former rate of pay.

However, among the variety of specified program priorities, such as target group, occupational/other training, participant support, all of them general and inclusive, there was a "program model priority" which gave state focus to this program. That was "training and program design with preference to consortia or cooperative arrangements." The focus was on the structure through which the program grants operated. GETO wanted agencies to work together in a coordinated approach to assure a broad array of services, one of the distinctive features of the Dane County project.

With its emphasis on providing a full range of services through a cooperative or consortia arrangement, the state, in distributing the RFP funded Title III monies, influenced program mix only in the sense that it required the full mix to be available. There was emphasis that any skill training or OJT lead to real employment at the end of the process.

Further, the state set specific performance goals. Programs must achieve reasonable program outcomes for the following measures: (a) a placement rate of 60 percent; (b) cost per entered employment of less than $4,000; (c) an average wage at placement of 85 percent of preprogram wage; and (d) a job retention rate of 90 percent after six months.

Priority in this project was to be given to laid-off Giddings & Lewis workers, steelworkers union members whose wage ($9.00/hr., $4.00 fringe) is considerably above the wages of the occupations in Dane County in which they are likely to find employment. They are generally skilled workers. However, they accounted for only 54 of the 218 served in this program.

The Nature of the Project

Over 55 Employment Service, Inc., is the recipient of the Title III grant. There is a unique arrangement which allows Over 55 to be the grant recipient and provide services, but the program impetus, design, implementation, and operational management have been handled by a group calling itself the Title III Consortium. The Consortium is made up of the three largest and most respected Community-Based Organizations in Dane County. This group includes Over 55 Employment Service, Inc., Project Fresh Start (PFS), and Employment and Training Association (ETA). These groups have over 40 years combined experience providing employment and training services in Dane County.

Although Over 55 is the grant recipient, this does not connote any special role for that agency in program operations except that it provides the recordkeeping and houses the compliance materials.

Over 55 subcontracts with ETA and PFS for services to participants; each agency is responsible for enrolling its own participants. Each organization has a recognized expertise in addressing different types of problems. It is not unusual for participants to be referred to one of the other agencies in the group for more appropriate services. A coordinator is responsible for keeping the three operators informed about enrollment and placement issues, and for chairing a monthly meeting between the groups to keep in touch with overall program goals, objectives, and problem areas.

These agencies have an interesting experience with older workers. Over 55, as the name implies, has always served older workers. It has not always received CETA or JTPA funds, but has helped older people secure employment. The other agencies also have target groups to whom they are recognized service providers. Fresh Start has traditionally served young people with multiple problems, such as drug or alcohol users, offenders, and school dropouts. It also serves women, but has difficulty attracting them to the program. Employment and Training Association has served a wide variety of people, but is most closely identified with welfare mothers and General Assistance recipients.

A number of people on the board of Fresh Start and ETA questioned the wisdom of securing funds to serve people laid off from Giddings and Lewis and others who fit the traditional view of a Title III participant. Both agency directors were anxious to expand Title III participation. They saw the more open eligibility criteria for Title III as an opportunity to provide service to other groups. They were able to convince their boards of the wisdom of their plan. The groups had come together to apply for the Title III funds before the Giddings and Lewis closing was announced. The plant provided a public relations vehicle to ensure that this project would be funded.

This program was conceived to strengthen linkages within the Dane County service delivery area. The three major service providers, former competitors, came together to present a comprehensive plan to the state that would utilize the strengths of all three agencies, as well as other service providers in the area. All three believe that an individual approach to the participants' particular needs and goals is most effective. They set up the program to allow the operators to contract with the service provider in the area who could best meet those needs.

The SDA, while not involved in the planning or operation of the program, supported the proposal initially and allowed the consortium to enter the participant and financial data on their computers. In the second year of the project, this was provided at no cost to the program. The program also had contracts for basic education at the technical school. They would also pay for slots at the technical school or at some private schools in the community. The coordination process was simple. After a participant completed the assessment process, the agency would contract with the necessary service delivery agents to complete the program.

The state required all Title III operators to use Job Service for Title III certification. All three grantees agreed that this was the one linkage that didn't work. These agencies are used to doing their own certification and found the state service to be expensive, inaccurate, and cumbersome for the agencies and participants.

The project is a communitywide effort to serve the Title III eligible population. During the RFP evaluation process at the state level, Giddings and Lewis, a multinational corporation, announced that it was closing its Madison foundry facility which employed over 100 people. The timing was good for the local proposal. It gave some immediacy to the proposal and ensured its funding, but the program was not specifically designed to serve this particular group. In fact, the proposal was altered to include the people laid off from Giddings and Lewis, but there were no programmatic alterations made because of this addition. The project became known as the Giddings and Lewis program, even though only 54 of the 218 participants were from that plant.

There were no other firms that had a block of participants like Giddings and Lewis but the participants did come from interesting industry segments. Dane County has been experiencing a major battle in the grocery business; several chains have been bought and sold with adverse effects on the workers in this industry. The purchase of a local retail drugstore chain also adversely affected their local employees. Both of these groups were being served by the project. Also included were laid-off workers from state and local government, the largest local employer.

No particular industries were targeted for placement because the project was designed to individualize placement goals for each participant.

In Madison, however, the insurance and retail areas were growing, while government and manufacturing were declining.

The program has been implemented as proposed. The group has made one budget modification based upon their experience in placement activities. Money had been budgeted for OJT contracts with employers, but they found that employers were willing to take Title III participants without the on-the-job training incentive. Instead of wasting time trying to sell OJT, they modified the grant, reducing funds for OJT and adding another placement person to the staff. The change has worked well, as they have exceeded their placement goals.

The people served by the program are served on a first come first served basis although priority is given to participants who have a number of barriers to employment and to any worker laid off from Giddings and Lewis.

The Consortium did attempt to centralize the job club function with one agency but they were not happy with the results. The counselors working with the participants felt the ongoing relationship was important and, therefore, each agency continued its own placement and job club activities.

The private sector played no real role in the design, implementation or delivery of services involved in the operation of this program. However, the private sector is critical to the program's placement efforts.

The Giddings and Lewis personnel department did provide access during working hours, for the purpose of Title III certification, to the people who were to be laid off. It also gave each employee a typed one-page sheet which included biographical information and job skills. This information was helpful in putting together resumes for the people from Giddings and Lewis. The effort lasted only until the plant was actually closed. The Consortium had asked for a cash contribution to the program and were told it was under consideration. Shortly after the plant closed, they were told the company had decided against any financial contribution.

The members of the Consortium were unanimous in their opinion that the private sector does not have a role in designing this type of program except at the hiring end. "Employers have said to us, 'give us people who show up, want to work hard, and have good attitudes and we will train them. We don't need OJT subsidies or other JTPA incentives.' " Although the agencies have private sector representatives on their boards and employer advisory committees, these are really for public relations and placement value rather than substantive input to the design of the program.

The Steelworkers Union and the Madison Federation of Labor have played an active and supportive role in the implementation and opera-tion of the Title III program. The Steelworkers union hall was used for job club and job search activities. The Steelworkers Union presi-dent actively encouraged his members to participate. The Federation of Labor, the local union umbrella organization, actively supported the initial grant and its renewal. The Federation has been an excellent source of referrals and outreach activities for the program. All the efforts of the Federation were undertaken without any reimbursement.

The union was criticized for its efforts surrounding the Giddings and Lewis closing. The Federation led an effort to explore the feasibility of selling the foundry and continuing its operation. Some people thought that this effort had raised false hopes among the foundry workers. The buy-out prospect, according to these critics, was never feasible. Because it was an issue in the press, however, it enabled the workers to put off confronting the reality that their jobs were ending and that they could not expect to get jobs paying the same wage rates that they had receiv-ed for the past 10 to 20 years.

Program Services

A wide variety of services are provided by this project. Each person is assessed and a plan is developed for that individual. The plan may include any of a wide variety of placement activities, from direct place-ment assistance, to job clubs, to job seeking skill training, to employ-ment counseling. Of the 250 people who registered for the program,

210 received employment counseling. This could be as minimal as assistance with an employability plan to ongoing counseling and placement. Job seeking skills training was provided, including resume writing to 154 participants, while 195 of the 218 enrollees were referred to job openings. Seven participants asked for in-depth assessment services. Seventeen people enrolled in basic education classes. OJT contracts were written for only 10 people. Sixty-five participants enrolled in some form of classroom training.

There is no service sequence in the project. Everyone must agree to look for work with a placement person and on their own. Some training classes have particular entry requirements, but these are detailed in the assessment process. Some people wanted to continue their education but needed a GED or wanted some adult basic education (ABE) courses as a tryout to see if they could handle going to school. Some of the ABE people did then move on to specific training.

The program has a heavy emphasis on individual needs. If one accepts that thesis and looks at the services chosen by participants, it is clear that the participants were most anxious to go to work. They used the placement assistance that they believed would provide employment as soon as possible.

According to the program operators, the Giddings and Lewis people were the most confused and reluctant about job seeking. Unemployment compensation alone provides over $5.00 per hour in Wisconsin. The Giddings and Lewis people were adamant about wanting jobs paying from $6.50 to $10.00 per hour plus benefits. Some of this masked a fear of looking for work, because most of these people had been working in the same place for 10 to 20 years. As it happened, the first person in the group to get a job as a janitor, at $5.75 per hour with full benefits, was a likable fellow who, it was said, was not the brightest person in the group. The feeling was, "If he could land that type of job, so can we." The job search interest picked up considerably after this fellow went to work.

The kinds of training provided were again on an individualized basis. The OJT slots were as follows:

Gilson Electronics	Sub assembler
Lessner Cabinet	Cabinet makers
McFarland Schools	Custodian
Wisconsin Power & Light	Clerical
WISCO Industries	Punch press operator
Electric Motor Co.	Salesman

The classroom program provided training in the following areas:

Class	Participants
Truck Driving	1
Word Processing	10
Janitorial Maintenance	4
Accounting	1
Intro to Computers	8
Starting Your Own Small Business	8
Graphic Design	1
Principles of Real Estate	1
Real Estate Law	1
Financial Management	1
Data Processing	3
Electronics	1
Nursing	1
Hotel Management	1

The only difference in this list of training selections by participants and a group of Title IIA participants in a similarly designed program is the large group of people in the course, "Starting Your Own Small Business." All the people in the course were from the Giddings and Lewis foundry. It is clear that these people were reacting to losing long-term jobs. As it worked out, five of the people who took the course left the program as nonpositive terminations.

Counseling is an extremely important part of this project. It consists not only of the traditional counselor-client relationship, but also the project organized a variety of other vehicles for counseling. There were small group sessions each week to share experiences and progress. They held large group meetings to ensure feedback to the program operators. The job search skills were most important and were provided in a variety of ways. There were structured classes teaching job seeking skills and assisting with resumes and interviewing techniques. There were job clubs which included group support, interview practice and help with the telephone. There were individual counselors who would work one on one with people who felt uncomfortable about working in group settings.

Counseling experienced workers about the availability of jobs that pay below their previous wage was difficult but important. Madison has the lowest unemployment rate in the state. It is the state capital, and over 30,000 government workers are employed there. It was hard but important for the participants to see their co-workers take jobs at lower pay levels, in order to make it acceptable for everyone to do so.

Counseling for personal problems was also available and in steady demand. One of the subcontractors, Project Fresh Start, dealt with the people's personal problems, working with those who had alcohol, drug, or other personal problems. Their method has had great success. For example, the organization purchases homes in disrepair so that the Title III participants may be assigned to a work crew to fix up and refurbish the house. The crew leader is not only a skilled craftsman, but also has had counseling training. The crew fixes up the home and sells it to a low income family. This work discipline and support enables people with multiple problems to feel good about themselves and begin a serious job search.

Participant Characteristics

The participants in this program come from a wide variety of occupations. The single largest employer was the Giddings and Lewis plant that closed. Fifty-four of the 218 served were from Giddings and Lewis. Professional and administrative was the next largest group with 39 participants. Included in this group were a number of state, local and federal government workers, nurses laid off from local hospitals, and mid-management people from Ohio Medical, another take-over victim.

Clerical workers included 17 from government, Oscar Mayer, and other smaller employers. There were also a number of workers laid off from Eagles, Kohls, or Sentry (food stores) taking part in the program.

Participants are enrolled on a first come first served basis except for the Giddings and Lewis employees. If there was an enrollment conflict, priority was given to employees with the most barriers to employment. Previous occupations of participants are shown in table 10-3. Characteristics of terminees are shown in table 10-4.

Table 10-3
Prior Occupations, Dane County Program

Job category	Participants number	Percent
Professional, administrative	39	18
Clerical	17	8
Housekeeping, cleaning	1	—
Drivers, deliveries	2	—
Food services	9	4
Maintenance, janitorial	15	7
Skilled trades	73[a]	34
Sales, retailing	11	5
Production work	12	6
Miscellaneous[b]	35	16
Total	214	

a. Fifty-four from Giddings and Lewis.

b. Includes categories such as greenskeeper, service station operator, printer, dairy farmer.

Program Outcomes

This Title III project is probably characterized by a unique program model, one which can be viewed as nontraditional, though one which is probably a reasonable model for the use of the Title III monies in areas which are not heavily industrial and do not display large populations of dislocated workers as envisioned by the drafters or JTPA Title III.

The problem this project sets out to address is that of secondary, or hidden, displaced workers. As the major blue-collar employers in Dane

Table 10-4
Enrollment and Participants Characteristics
from March 1, 1984 to December 31, 1984

Selected characteristics	Number	Percent
Total participants	218	
Total terminations	154	
Entered employment	119	77[a]
Other positive terminations	10	6
Other terminations	25	16
Sex		
Male	159[b]	73
Female	59	27
Age		
14–15	—	—
16–19	—	—
20–21	—	—
22–44	108	62
45–54	58	27
55 and over	52	24
Education		
School dropout	42	19
School (H.S. or less)	0	—
High school graduate or more	158	72
Race		
White	191	88
Black	24	11
Hispanic	2	1
Native American	0	—
Asian	1	*
Employment barriers		
Limited English	3	1
Handicapped	32	14
Offender	24	11
Other	—	—
Benefit recipiency		
U.I. claimant	100[c]	46
U.I. exhaustee	44	20
Public assistance (GA)	50	23
AFDC	6	3
Youth AFDC	—	—
Labor force status (prior 26 weeks)		
Unemployed 1–14 weeks	NA	
Unemployed 15 or more weeks	NA	
Not in labor force	NA	

NOTE: The tables in this report do not match precisely because the program operator and the state showed slightly different enrollment and placement counts.

a. 81 percent without Giddings and Lewis.

b. 104 males minus the 54 males from Giddings and Lewis.

c. Filed: 58; receiving: 42.

*Less than .5 percent.

NA – Information not available.

County curtail operations or shut down altogether, there is a population of workers who, while not directly employed at the affected plants, find themselves laid off in the rippling of the primary layoffs, throughout the community. These employees, from restaurants, bars, retail and service shops of various kinds, are no less displaced workers, but are not so concentrated and not so visible. As discussed previously, there is also an emerging population of displaced workers who are casualties of take-overs, buyouts, and private sector reorganizations. Moving these individuals back into employment is the problem to which this project intended to respond. In addition, the more traditional group of Giddings and Lewis males happened to come along during the funding process. The principal population does not look very different from the Title IIA population generally served, but is somewhat older, has held jobs successfully, and holds in common the process by which they had lost those jobs.

The project has generally done what it set out to do. Because of the project and the level at which it was funded, it could not provide retraining to everyone if they all wanted it. But the project has brought Title III monies into the county, served a somewhat different population from what these agencies usually see, and has overseen their movement back into employment at a very respectable rate, for both the initial population and the Giddings and Lewis group. The agencies serve as a labor market mediator and advocate for the persons enrolled and provide a protected and caring place during the bewildering journey between a job loss unrelated to personal performance and securing new employment.

We seem to have here an imaginative and credible, if limited, approach to pulling Title III monies into an area where traditional displaced workers are few, and using those funds to assist secondary displaced workers into employment. However, the frustrations born of this limited approach are apparent. One operator said, "We've done our part. People are motivated, ready to work. But where are the jobs?" There is also the observation that some displaced workers do not feel successful because of the quality of the job they've managed to find.

Specific program outcome information, where applicable, in relation to the state performance standards, is shown in table 10-5.

Table 10-5
Program Outcomes, Dane County Project

Outcome information	Standard	Actual total	Giddings and Lewis only
Enrolled	—	214	54
Placed	—	119	30
Placement rate	60%	74%	68%
Wage on prior job	—	$6.93	$9.06[1]
Wage at placement	$5.79	$5.81	$6.19
(85% of pre-program)			
Wage replacement rate	85%	84%[2]	68%
Cost per placement	$4,000	$1,551	—

1. Plus $4.00 fringe benefits.
2. For the total minus Giddings and Lewis, this figure was 88 percent.

Overall Assessment

The individualized approach utilizes a wide variety of placement strategies. There is a lot of encouragement for individual job search with the assistance from a job coach. There is also some job development done for individual participants. The agencies staff felt that the biggest hurdle to overcome was and is the wage expectations of the participants, particularly those from Giddings and Lewis.

There is little, if any, placement done by prior agreement with particular employers. Placement activity appears excellent with 119 placements for the 218 participants. Only 25 people terminated nonpositively, 14 from Giddings and Lewis. According to program staff, over half of the nonpositive terminees were older workers who decided to leave the labor force and live on savings or other income.

Relocation is not used as a placement strategy. Madison has the lowest unemployment rate in the state. Very few workers expressed interest in relocation. The union president, however, did think that more effort should be directed at exploring employment opportunities at the prior wage scales in a much larger geographic area.

There are several groups in the eligible population for this project and the appropriateness and relative effectiveness of the project's approach differs for the various groups. There are a traditional group of dislocated workers from Giddings and Lewis; a group of secondary displaced workers who are younger with shorter work histories, and less investment in their former firm; and in both groups, older workers with few work years left, and younger workers closer to the beginning of their work lives.

For all these subsets, the first role of these agencies is to break the news to them, in terms they can understand, of the realities of today's labor market. They will *not* be working at the same wage and benefit level immediately and perhaps not for a very long time, if ever. The burden of actually bringing the bad news, which is going to fall somewhat differentially on the subsets, resides with these agencies.

This kind of program is a resource that can support people through frightening times. However, it is unique among those resources, because it is targeted and it is intended to go beyond income support to assist people to get back into a job. Because of the variety of problems, it was appropriate that this consortium attempted an approach which, while principally job matching, does have some flexibility to permit everything from long-term training for some who are interested to intensive job search assistance for those who want immediate employment.

NOTE

1. Giddings and Lewis has now closed permanently.

11
Findings and Conclusions

The case studies included in this volume were not chosen to be representative of the universe of projects being operated under Title III of JTPA. Rather, they represent projects with different forms of organization, providing varied services to diverse populations of dislocated workers. The only commonality is that they were thought to be successful program models by state and local program staff. As noted in the introduction, the purpose of this volume is to present some of the lessons learned from these studies that may be of use to those interested in employment and training policy and to operators of Title III projects.

Overall, these projects, despite some individual problems, were generally successful. Table 11-1 shows the outcomes of the individual case studies for the placement rate of terminees, the cost per placement, and the wage replacement ratio for individuals placed. For comparison, the table also presents the average results on the same variables for the six Dislocated Worker Demonstration Projects funded with fiscal year 1983 CETA money.

Success, measured in comparison to the average for the CETA demonstrations, is obviously relative. That the JTPA projects are defined as successful does not mean they meet the objectives of section 106 of the Act—to increase long-term earnings of the participants beyond what they would have been without the program. Rather, the measures being used are short-term indicators of success. To determine the long-term impact of the program, it would be necessary to have a control group or observe the counterfactual outcome. That is, what proportion

193

Table 11-1
Case Study Project Outcomes

Projects	Size	Placement rate (percent)	Cost per placement	Wage replacement ratio (percent)
Cummins Engine Company	708	83	$3,732	69
GM-UAW Metroplitan Pontiac PREP	2,189	93	$900-$1,000	NA
Minnesota Iron Range	1,324	62	$863	62
Missouri Job Search Assistance, Inc.	963	78	$1,023	83
Cone-Mills Project	360	98[b]	NA	86
United Labor Agency	1,083	60+[c]	$829-$906	89
Houston Community College	855	74	$1,735	71
Tacoma Copper Smelter	366	85	$1,240	78
Dane County, Wisconsin	218	60	$4,000	85
Dislocated worker demonstrations under CETA[a]	1,040	55	$2,324	70

a. *Serving the Dislocated Worker: A Report on the Dislocated Worker Demonstration Program.* Abt Associates, Inc., U.S. Department of Labor, Employment and Training Administration, Washington, D.C., December 1983. Figure 4.1 and table IV.11. Placement rates were recalculated to include recalls based on data from the individual case studies.

b. This excluded a number of individuals (130) in a "service" category. If these individuals are included, the placement rate would be 63 percent.

c. The official placement rate (45 percent) only includes placements at $5.25 or more per hour.

of these dislocated workers would have been placed in employment and what wages would they have received in the absence of the program.

All of the case study projects had placement rates higher than the average for the CETA-funded demonstrations. An apparent exception, the United Labor Agency Project in Cleveland, Ohio, had a lower reported placement rate because only individuals placed at wages above the performance standard for the state ($5.25 per hour) were counted as placed. If placements at lower wage rates were included, the placement rate for that project would have exceeded 60 percent.

At the same time, the Hillsborough Cone-Mills project, with a reported placement rate of 98 percent, excludes 130 individuals who were in what was called the "service" category, which is, essentially, individual job search following program services. If these individuals are considered to have been terminated but not placed, the placement rate for this project would drop to 63 percent, above the average for the CETA demonstrations, but not as positive as the project's statistics would suggest.

Two of the case study sites, the Cummins Engine Company and Dane County projects, had costs above the average for the demonstrations ($2,324 per placement). However, the average cost for the Dislocated Worker Demonstrations excludes two sites that, for specific reasons, had very high costs (Southgate and Alameda). Further, the cost per placement in the Cummins Engine Company project is biased upward by the large number of individuals who were still in the project. The cost per placement for the Cone-Mills project could not be estimated because it was part of a statewide program.

Finally, among the case studies for which a wage replacement ratio could be calculated, only two had ratios below the average for the CETA demonstrations. It is interesting to note that both of these cases, the Cummins Engine Company and Minnesota Iron Range projects, involved layoffs in the major high-wage industry in an otherwise rural and low-wage area.

Project Targeting

Probably the most obvious point about program targeting, evident in the Pontiac Retraining and Employment Program, is the determination of who is truly a displaced, as opposed to a cyclically unemployed, worker. Early discussion of the number of dislocated workers in the nation had to do with the separation of these populations. The number of dislocated workers was variously estimated from 300,000 to 5.1 million people.

It appears that something closer to the smaller number is probably more accurate. A large number of technically dislocated workers have, in fact, been recalled to their old jobs or have found employment in variations of them. Not only was this the case in the Pontiac project, another potential project was dropped from the study sample when the entire eligible population had been recalled by the time the project was organized. Further, 10 percent of the terminees in the CETA Dislocated Worker Demonstrations were recalled by their previous employers. This suggests that better targeting of programs by the states is needed to avoid spending money on people who will eventually return to their previous employer. As noted in the Pontiac case study, "it is possible that the potential participants had a better idea of the probability of being recalled than did the employment and training professionals." For these workers, extended unemployment benefits or income maintenance may be more appropriate than training. The policy problem is, of course, to identify them ahead of time—project targeting.

The specific targeting of the projects also varied. The Hillsborough, ASARCO, and Pontiac projects were plant-specific, and, in the latter two cases, also union member-specific. Under these circumstances, the targeting was fairly clear-cut and initial screening excluded those who were not in the specific target group. However, in the case of the Hillsborough project, a small proportion of the participants were not from the Cone-Mills plant; this is the result of the ripple effects of the closing of the largest plant in the local community.

With the exception of the ASARCO project, there was no project that ended up being 100 percent plant- or industry-specific. With this exception, in cases in which a particular plant or a particular industry was targeted, the project also eventually served people from the community who were adversely affected by the primary dislocation in the area. In the case of the Hillsborough Cone-Mills project, affected individuals from the local economy were served. In the case of the Minnesota Iron Range project, people from the local community as well as spouses of the iron miners and the children of both groups who were attempting to find work upon graduation from high school were served—the latter two groups with the SDA's Title IIA funds.

In those cases in which the targeting was on all Title III eligibles within a geographic area, there was no screening problem beyond the determination of eligibility, though in these cases the mix of services had to be more varied to deal with the differing skill levels of the participants.

Many eligible people dislocated from a given plant never come in. Although the Cummins Engine Company was the source of the largest number of layoffs in the three-county area, only 17 percent of the participants in the project were from Cummins. This supports the Cummins' contention that the project was really designed to serve the entire community, but also underscores the fact that many of the workers from a particular plant either wait for recall, retire, or find other opportunities without the aid of a project. In the Cummins project, program operation began two and one-half years after the workers were laid off. Consequently, the majority of those workers had to find other employment without the services provided by the Title III project.

This also appears to be the case in the ASARCO project. Of the 600 laid off, 118 took early retirements and 366 enrolled in the project. One-fifth of the eligibles never came in. In all of the case study sites, older workers who had supplementary benefits or the ability to "hang on" until retirement never participated in the projects. Few members of the older segment of the eligible population are served by these programs, even though the proportion of older participants tends to be higher than in Title IIA programs.

In unionized industries that have negotiated supplementary unemployment benefits, individuals who have these benefits may attempt to wait until they are convinced that the plant will not recall them or until they run out of benefits. If the project opens its doors immediately, lower enrollments than planned may result. Until it is obvious that the plant will not be reopened or the recall notices will not come, senior workers may not be willing to participate in the program. Furthermore, when Unemployment Insurance, Trade Adjustment payments, Supplementary Unemployment Benefits and severance pay amount to 50 to 70 percent of previous take home pay, there may be little inclination to participate in a program that promises employment with an expected wage replacement rate of 65 percent and concomitant loss of these benefits.

In the case of plant closings, it is possible to obtain advance notice and to set up the project in anticipation of the plant closing. Then, the potential dislocated workers can be identified, assessment performed, and a program tailored to the needs of the eligible population can be designed. In the case of major layoffs, such action is generally not possible. Because of the possible effects on the morale of the employees, companies are not inclined to announce layoffs ahead of time. Advance notice of plant closings may assist in the design of the project but may adversely affect the production of the plant. In the Hillsborough plant, 130 people left or retired in the period between the announcement of the closing and the time when the plant actually closed. While this may be disruptive to the company, it reduces the number of individuals to be served by the project.

In the case of the ASARCO project, virtually all employees stayed to the end. This may have been quite rational in terms of the relative wage levels and the condition of the labor market in the area. Also, unlike the Hillsborough project, unemployment and supplementary unemployment benefits, as well as severance pay, were contingent upon holding on until the closure. The history of the industry also held the hope that the "gates might reopen."

Intake and Selection

In the six CETA-funded Dislocated Worker Demonstrations, differences in recruitment practices between projects which had a target group of workers from specific plants and projects which served all Title III eligibles in the community were observed. In the former case, companies and unions were willing to assist in the identification of, and contacts with, laid-off workers. In the latter case, a less structured procedure of public announcements through radio, television and newspaper advertisements was the most common method for making contact with eligible unemployed workers.

Differences are also observed in the recruitment practices of projects included in these case studies. In cases where the target group was plant- or industry-specific (the Hillsborough, Michigan PREP, Minnesota Iron Range and ASARCO projects), local project staff involved management or the labor union in the recruitment of eligible workers. This was also true in the Dane County and United Labor Agency projects.

For example, the program staff of the Hillsborough project received a master list of laid-off employees from the personnel department of the Cone-Mills plant, which was used as a mailing list. The master list was also a means of checking eligibility for the program, and a way of defining the primary target group to give them priority for program services. In addition, management posted program information around the plant and paid for radio and newspaper advertisements. In the Pontiac project, the UAW and General Motors provided project staff with the names and addresses of all laid-off auto workers with recall rights, i.e., the target group for the project. In the ASARCO project, announcements, intake and assessment were completed in the plant before its closing.

Recruitment of eligibles in cases where the target group for the project was not plant-specific primarily relied on print and television media. In Missouri and Indiana, for example, program operators attempted to recruit through advertisements.

None of the projects experienced any buildup problems, although some, such as the Cummins project, experienced lower numbers of applications than anticipated and never really had an applicant pool. However, involvement of management and labor unions in recruitment efforts does facilitate immediate contact with the eligible population and also adds to the credibility of the program. The only other project that experienced recruitment problems relied on "walk-ins" and a computer system designed to generate the name, phone number and occupational code for UI claimants and exhaustees.

If the target group is laid-off workers from a plant closing, as in the ASARCO project, recruitment can begin before layoff. Recruitment is more difficult when the plant or union has lost contact with the workers. In the Pontiac project, for instance, recruitment did not begin until five years after the first layoffs occurred. As a result, 30 percent of the laid-off workers could not be located by mail.

In the Cummins case study, although the Cummins plant accounted for almost half of the 3,400 eligible dislocated workers, the fact that the layoffs had occurred two years before the project started was considered the primary reason why these workers constituted only 17 percent of the participants. The others presumably "found their own way."

If there is a large eligible population from which to select participants, as in the Minnesota Iron Range, Cleveland United Labor Agency, and Pontiac projects, almost any recruitment strategy will produce the desired number of applicants. In these cases, the more important question is how to build program enrollments without creating lengthy waiting periods between application, enrollment and service delivery for unemployed workers.

Assessment

The earlier Dislocated Worker Demonstrations involved prescreening based on education, attitudes and motivation to improve the probable placement success of the program. None of the programs observed for these case studies had any such screening procedure. For example, participants in the Cummins project were screened only to determine eligibility. Following eligibility verification, workers participated in a three-day assessment program to develop an employability plan. Participants then voluntarily enrolled in one of several program activities. As noted, this was because the advisory board wanted everyone to "go away with something," even those who did not choose to participate in any of the program services. In the case of the Job Search Assistance, Inc., (JSA) program in Missouri, intake sessions were scheduled based on the expectation of a certain number of eligibles coming in. Staff noted, however, that if more people than expected came in, they would simply increase the size of the job club.

Assessment was a major part of all projects observed in the case studies. Seven of the nine projects combined collection of information on participant work history, skill level, occupational interests and education with formal tests of aptitude and skill level. The other two projects included in their assessment work histories and skill levels as reported by the participants. All nine had some procedure for assessing the participants' skill needs, abilities and the types of training and jobs that might match their abilities and skills.

The results of the assessment and testing were used by most projects to develop, in varying degrees of formality, an employability plan. Counselors informed the participants of the test results, presented the service options, and discussed job possibilities. Choosing program activities was left to the participant, with counselors providing guidance. For example, in the Minnesota Iron Range project, results of the aptitude test were reviewed by the counselors, and participants were discouraged from entering training for which they lacked ability or aptitude.

The case studies suggest that assessment and testing were important parts of the program. While participants were allowed to express their interest in a particular plan or program activity, as in the ASARCO project, the counselors also had a role in those decisions.

Service Mix

The service mix in the case study projects is summarized in table 11-2. The information in the table is not completely comparable, because the services were defined differently in the different projects, particularly counseling, assessment and job search. For example, assessment may be the first activity in the job search skills segment of the job club, as is the case in the Job Search Assistance, Inc. project in Missouri. Another project may record that the participant received assessment only if money was expended specifically for formal assessment, as in the case of the United Labor Agency project in Cleveland. However, even with these limitations, several points emerge from the table.

Most obviously, although the emphasis and primary services provided by the projects vary, no project offered only a single service, such as job search. This was true even in the case of the Job Search Assistance, Inc. project in Missouri. Although JSA originally had to be pressured by the state to use OJT, project staff indicated that the more comprehensive program improved their placement results. Similarly, those projects that emphasized assessment and counseling (the United Labor Agency project and the Dane County project) also made training services available to participants.

Two more points emerge from all of the case studies. First, all had flexibility built into the service mix of the projects. Second, all gave free choice to the participants in choosing among the available services. In every case, a worker was free to enroll in a particular part of the program. This was, of course, subject to availability and sometimes, as with the Houston Community College-Texas Employment Commission project, to the requirement that individuals go through a job search component as the initial program activity. Though often combined with mandatory assessment and screening, however, the degree of voluntarism is striking.

One constraint on available services is the willingness of contractors to take performance-based contracts, exemplified by the JSA project in Missouri. However, even where there are no performance-based con-

Table 11-2
Services Enrollment in (percentages) Title III Dislocated Worker Project Case Studies

Total/Service	Cummins Engine Company	GM-UAW Pontiac PREP	Minnesota Iron Range	Job Search Assistance Missouri	Cone-Mills Hillsborough N. Carolina	United Labor Agency	Houston Community College	ASARCO Project	Dane County
Total participants	708	2,189	1,324	963	360	1,083	855	366	218
Service									
Counseling and Assessment	All	All	8	*	*	68	All	All	96
Job Search	—	—	25	—	88	71	—	200	89
Job Club	63	5	23	100	—	—	All	—	—
Classroom Training	26	23	23	—	14	14	24	221	30
OJT	6	—	6	17	17	12	7	3	5
Adult Basic Education	—	—	11	—	14	—	—	—	8
Relocation	—	—	9	—	—	—	—	2	—
Orientation	—	—	—	—	—	—	—	All	—
Work Experience	—	—	—	—	—	1	—	—	—

*Counseling and assessment provided in Job Search Assistance or Job Club.

tracts, the use of particular contractors depends upon their prior track record, as in the Minnesota Iron Range, Cummins and Dane County projects.

A further example of this kind of flexibility is illustrated in the Pontiac project. A small but significant part of this program was assessment, counseling and job search assistance for 75 eligible individuals who did not want to return to the auto industry. It was suggested that this program might be provided at the time of layoff to individuals who choose to change occupations rather than continue in a boom and bust industry.

Another point is that only in the case of the Minnesota Iron Range and ASARCO projects, where they were backed by state Title III funds, were project officials willing to support long-term large-scale institutional training. This, of course, was stimulated in these cases by the nature of the local labor market. In the other projects, one-year funding and pressure from the Department of Labor to spend the funds led to a concentration on short-term strategies and job search. In the Cleveland United Labor Agency project, both project staff and the case study author indicated that, had they been able to provide longer term training in advanced technology, a growing industry in the Cleveland-Cuyahoga County labor market, they could have increased their placement and wage replacement percentages.

The other source of pressure for short-term services, best illustrated by the Hillsborough Cone-Mills project, is the clear preference among dislocated workers for immediate income and, therefore, for job search and on-the-job training as opposed to classroom training. This is particularly true where completion of training holds no definite promise of a job.

Expenditures under Title III have consistently run below budget, while the number of individuals served has been above projections. Almost all of these projects have run a job search or job club program as the first service, because dislocated workers, although they may have skills, have not been in the job market for a number of years and are not familiar with resume writing or the procedures for finding a job. As one author put it, they are accustomed to "come in today, show up for work tomorrow" hiring procedures.

Relation to the Labor Market

The appropriateness of the project to the labor market is illustrated in the Cummins project. Staff there started by adopting the Downriver project's strategy of relying on job search assistance. However, the Downriver project involved several plant closings in an area with a substantial number of similar firms not experiencing layoffs and took place early in the recession. Therefore, job search was appropriate as the major service. The utility of transferring this model to southern Indiana, where the major industry was the Cummins plant and the firms that supply it represented a rather different labor market, is not immediately obvious. In fact, the Cummins project had to revise its program model to retrain dislocated workers for job openings within the area.

All nine projects show that it is efficient to operate a job search component at the outset of a program, thereby reducing training costs for those who may be able to readily find a job. Such action raises the project's placement rates while reducing the cost per placement. The case studies also demonstrate that there may be certain services that are particularly appropriate to the Title III eligible population. Examples include the certification of existing skills, as in the Minnesota Iron Range project, and the use of technical skills from the previous job in a sales capacity, an effective strategy for dealing with relatively skilled workers in the case of the Houston Community College-Texas Employment Commission project. These cost efficient strategies may be applicable in other areas or projects. The ASARCO project, with its impressive outcome measures, is much closer to the Dislocated Worker project "model."

Counseling

Essentially, three types of counseling were provided in the projects. Although counseling and the emphasis on particular types of counseling vary among the projects, all provided personal and financial counseling; job search skills counseling; and counseling with regard to the labor market and wage expectations.

Many eligible dislocated workers, particularly those who have exhausted their unemployment benefits and savings, need financial counseling, including advice on debt consolidation, home equity loans, etc. Many long-term unemployed individuals also require counseling and referral to social service agencies for alcoholism or drug dependence, spouse or child abuse, welfare application, etc.

Many of these individuals, furthermore, have been employed for many years in the same firm and need counseling regarding job search skills: how to prepare a resume, how to efficiently look for a job, how not to be adversely affected by rejection, how to get by the personnel staff or secretary to the person who makes the hiring decision, etc. Even though these individuals are experienced and have marketable skills, they may lack knowledge of how to package and present their experience. Providing this information is an important and cost effective way of promoting reemployment, particularly in combination with the retraining or certification of existing skills.

Labor market counseling, variously called "reality counseling," "wage and distance counseling," or "wage expectations counseling," was also important to this population. Many dislocated workers expect to find new jobs that pay as much or more than their previous job. Often they have been employed in the unionized sector of the labor force and expect to find the same wage levels in the nonunion labor market. More important, they have been in the "internal" labor market for many years and do not understand the "external" labor market. That is, they have to be made aware that a senior position within the firm is often posted for bids by employees of the firm. This position, once filled by someone from within the firm, then creates another vacancy that is also posted. The final job listed in the external labor market is often an entry level position.

Having been dislocted from an industry, they must now compete in the external market for entry level jobs and may not obtain a position similar to their previous job. This is hard to swallow for workers who think of themselves as responsible and well-paid employees of many years' experience, whether they are blue-collar or white-collar workers. In the Houston case study, it was harder for the white-collar workers to accept this fact than it was for the blue-collar employees.

Also, many workers do not want to commute to a new job, or to relocate to find employment. The necessity of commuting was evident in the Cummins and Cone-Mills projects, located in rural labor markets, and most evident in the case of the Minnesota Iron Range project, the only one to include a substantial relocation component.

Placement

Job development and placement activities were part of the re-employment strategies for all but one of the observed programs. In most projects, self-directed job search or job clubs were combined with job development. Placement was occasionally aided by the use of OJT contracts for participants who could not locate employment through the job search, job development, and placement efforts. For example, in the Job Search Assistance project in Missouri, participants would receive one to three weeks of structured job search assistance. At least 100 participants who did not locate employment after the first week of the job club were then placed in OJT slots.

Job placement activities varied across the projects. The Minnesota Iron Range project used the Employment Service job bank to generate job leads. Participants were also provided access to in-state and out-of-state WATS lines. In Houston, a Resource Service Center supported the job search through the program's mandatory job search workshop. Contacts were made by canvassing newspapers and through the Texas Employment Commission's computerized job bank.

In the only project that did not emphasize job development, the Pontiac PREP program, a two-week employability skills component gave job search assistance to former General Motors employees not wanting to return to the auto industry.

The most important point concerning the job development aspects of these programs was the link to the assessment, testing and counseling activities described above. This combination, along with the training provided, served to produce impressive placement rates at reasonable cost.

Another issue, illustrated in the Hillsborough Cone-Mills project, is the placement of individuals back into the industry from which they were laid off. While desirable in the short run, this may only put off the final day of reckoning in a declining industry, and may be the non-union equivalent of waiting for the plant to reopen.

Placement back into the same industry may produce high wage replacement ratios. If the skills are industry-specific, the worker may obtain a higher wage by returning to the same industry. On the other hand, it may only delay dislocation from a declining industry, particularly where there is a change in the technology of the industry. If the individual can obtain a job in the "old" industry but lacks the skills appropriate to the "new" industry, then the funds may have been spent on an individual who will again be dislocated.

Conclusions

The original conception of Title III contained an implicit program model—that dislocated workers had industry-specific skills which, as the result of technological change or world competition, had become obsolete. A substantial investment in retraining would therefore be required to make them employable. However, the inability to specify who was a dislocated worker led to the broad targeting of unemployed, experienced workers who were "unlikely to return to their previous industry or occupation."

The result was that significant flexibility was granted to states and program operators to define the eligible population and the services to be provided to them. State and local officials used the flexibility of specifying the target group for the program to respond to the political need to "do something" about the problem of plant closings or mass layoffs in their jurisdictions.

The flexibility in terms of the services to be provided to participants was also used by program officials to respond to the perceived "needs" of the eligible population for the projects. Although the ASARCO project probably comes closest to the model originally contemplated, one-third of the placements from that program did not require long-term institutional training.

This reflects two other aspects of worker dislocation. First, the skills of dislocated workers are not entirely firm-specific. Experienced workers, particularly in cyclical industries, may have skills outside their job that they rely upon in periods of layoff. Further, as exemplified by the Minnesota case study, they may have generic skills resulting from their previous jobs that only need to be certified and "marketed" to a potential employer. Second, experienced workers may feel the need to be employed and/or have a need for immediate income. Thus, they have a preference for services (job search or OJT) that result in immediate employment rather than in long-term training which may hold no direct promise of a job. Yet, by virtue of their tenure on their previous job, they may not have knowledge of the labor market, how to efficiently present their skills, or search for a job. Therefore, flexibility in terms of the program model and services provided is also seen as appropriate to serve the needs of this population.

The organization, target groups, services provided and placement strategies of the projects included in this volume varied widely, according to the cause of the dislocation, the nature of the eligible population, the labor market in which the project operated, the sources of funding, etc. The one commonality of the projects was that state officials and local program operators thought they were successful. That is, they responded to the plant closing or layoff that originated the project; they provided the services that the population eligible for the project wanted; and, they produced results in terms of placement rates and costs per participant that proved their success. As noted in the introductory chapter of this volume, state and local officials were, in every case, pleased to have national attention given to their program.

As noted at the outset of this chapter, the results of these projects, in terms of their longer term net impacts, remain to be determined. Such an evaluation would be of strategic national policy interest and important to the reauthorization of the Title III Dislocated Worker Program. However, it is probably safe to say that the state officials, local program operators, and dislocated workers served and placed by the projects covered in this volume would be unimpressed by the greater statistical significance of the results. Of significance is the fact that government responded to the local problem of worker dislocation.

APPENDIX
Case Study Evaluation of Selected
Title III Dislocated Worker Projects

Case Study Report Form

Due: November 1, 1984

State:_____

Title III Project:

_____

Associate:

_____

Introduction to the Report Form

The purpose of this project is to produce a series of short case studies of individual Title III dislocated worker projects. We have selected nine Title III projects for study. In doing so we have attempted to select the projects to represent a variety of circumstances such as: projects that are firm and industry specific as well as those that serve all Title III eligible individuals within a given labor market; those that provide a variety of services from job search to classroom training to OJT to counseling; those operating in different labor markets, from a declining industry in an otherwise thriving labor market to ones operating within a generally depressed labor market; and projects operated by different organizations and with different strategies for providing services to dislocated workers.

With only nine case studies it is not possible to describe the universe or the entire range of dislocated worker projects. We have chosen fairly large projects (500 to 1,000 participants during the year) that appear to be operating successfully but represent a range of different service strategies, target groups and labor market conditions. Therefore, the question to be addressed in these studies is one of relative effectiveness—that is, what type of services are appropriate under varying circumstances and for particular target groups and labor markets. In so doing we hope to investigate questions such as the following:

• DOL planned $6,000 per participant in Title III on the assumption that the need of dislocated workers was for substantial institutional retraining. Others (such as Marc Bendick) have argued that the primary service under Title III should be job search assistance or that the primary need among experienced workers is for job finding skills and counseling aimed at reducing wage expectations.

• Relocation may be appropriate in generally depressed labor markets but most studies have indicated that individual participants are not interested in relocation.

• Our earlier reports indicated that potential participants were interested in jobs (implying a reliance on job search and OJT) rather than classroom training. Yet, some projects are emphasizing classroom training through community colleges and vocational schools.

• While the six Title III demonstration projects indicated that postprogram wage levels averaged 60 to 75 percent of preprogram wage levels, the early Job Training Longitudinal Survey (JTLS) results indicate that postprogram wages are slightly higher than preprogram wage levels for Title III participants.

• Different projects may have different eligible populations that require different services. For example a plant shutdown may idle more experienced and older workers while a partial layoff may idle younger, less experienced workers who may be more like Title IIA (economically disadvantaged) eligible participants.

Consequently, what we plan is to convert your reports into a set of short case studies that attempt to address these issues of relative effectiveness. The product will be a series of authored case studies and an overall chapter that attempts to distill some answers to the relative effectiveness issues outlined above. As such it is not our purpose to discuss implementation issues in particular locations or to provide information that may reflect on individual program operations.

This Report Form is organized into six parts as follows:

Part I State Organization of Title III
Part II The Local Labor Market
Part III The Nature of the Project
Part IV Program Participants
Part V Program Outcomes
Part VI Overall Assessment

This Report Form is designed to collect information on Title III projects at both the State and program level. Part I of the Report Form addresses the State level information. At the State level the questions focus on: the administering agency for Title III; State allocation of Title III resources; and whether an effort was made to incorporate Title III in State policy by defining the target population and/or service mix. Part II is concerned with the description of the labor market in which the program operates and the labor market origins of the project. Part III describes the organization and operation of the project itself, the services it provides and the way in which these services are provided. Information will be sought on the type of program operator; the nature of the program model; the targeting criteria used; the program models or models employed and the degree of private sector involvement in the project. Part IV attempts to examine outcome information on the project in a consistent fashion. Part VI is for your overall assessment of the project, its appropriateness to the eligible population and the nature of the labor market in which it operates and the outcomes that are produced.

We are using a Report Form rather than a detailed case study outline on the theory that it will promote consistency in the coverage of each topic, make it easier for your to write and for us to edit into a 20 to 25 page case study. Therefore, in your responses to the questions in the Report Form please remember that your answers will be converted into a single narrative.

Associate_____

Project_____

Part I. State Organization of Title III

The projects that will be observed for this evaluation were funded with either FY83, Secretary's Discretionary, EJB, TY84 or PY84 funds. In a number of states the organizational arrangements for Title III varied by funding source (i.e., more detailed planning of TY84 dollars). Therefore, in your conversations with the State officials please be sure that the organizational arrangements discussed pertain to the funding source of the project being observed.

1. What State agency is the organizational unit responsible for Title III? Briefly describe this agency's administrative position in the State bureaucracy (i.e., is there direct access to the governor). Are there separate agencies for Title III and Title IIA? Does one agency handle funding decisions and another the administration of the program, etc.? Is there a particular State focus to the program (e.g., economic development, support of services provided by Employment Security to dislocated workers, or emphasis on union/company operated programs)?

2. How did the administering agency distribute Title III resources for the fiscal year in which the project you are observing was funded? Was a Statewide program established; was the money distributed through a RFP process; or, was the money formula-funded, at least partially, to particular SDAs? If a RFP process was used, please indicate the criteria used as a basis for awarding grants. If the money was formula-funded, please describe the within-State formula.

3. Did the State establish Statewide Title III eligibility criteria or were such decisions left to the discretion of program operators? Did the State establish particular targeting goals or priorities for funding proposals? Were there any specific requirements with regard to a particular firm, industry, geographic area, or occupation?

4. Is there any indication that the State tried to influence the mix of services for its Title III programs? Please explain. Did the Governors special services plan impose any service requirements on Title III operators? How was a dislocated worker defined in this State, for this project? Does the State have any performance standards for Title III projects?

Part II. The Local Labor Market

1. Please discuss the nature of the local labor market (and define its area). What is the unemployment rate in the area? Are there particular plant closings? Is the labor market generally depressed? Are there particular growth areas or industries within the labor market? Is the area characterized by manufacturing or service industries; public or private sector jobs? (Of interest here are unemployment rates, sector breakdown of employment, plant closings in the last two years, degree of unionization, average wage rates, etc.)

2. Please describe the eligible population for this project in terms of the local labor market. For example, are only workers from a given plant, their spouses, or people affected in the local economy, any long-term unemployed individual, etc. eligible? Are they union members? Were their prior wage levels above the average in the local economy? Are they skilled or unskilled?

Part III. The Nature of the Project

1. Project Administration – What agency or organization is the recipient of the Title III grant? Does this agency actually run the program or do they subcontract program operations? What is this organization's experience in operating employment and training (or retraining) programs; have they had experience with older or more experienced workers? Who are the major subcontractors who actually provide the services?

2. Are there linkages with other parts of the employment and training system in the area (for example, the local SDA, the Employment Service, community colleges, vocational-technical schools, private training organizations, union or employer training programs, trade adjustment assistance, etc.)? If so how are these programs coordinated (actually vs. nominally)?

3. Please provide an overall description of the project. Are particular individuals targeted for service? What industries do the participants come from and what industries/firms are targeted for placement of participants postprogram? What services are to be provided (e.g., job search, OJT, etc.)?

4. How was this particular project chosen relative to other projects? Was it in response to the needs of the local labor market as described previously? What was the motivation of the State in approving the project or recommending it for discretionary Federal money?

5. Has the project been implemented as proposed or have changes been made in light of the reality of the situation? What kind of choices have been made concerning those in the eligible population who will be served (e.g., older vs. younger workers)? Has the service mix been adjusted (e.g., OJT and Job Search vs. long-term classroom training, job search skills and remedial education added, relocation services included or dropped, personal and labor market counseling added, etc.)?

6. Please discuss the nature and level of private sector involvement in the program. What local private sector actors (if any) play a role in the planning and implementation of the project? Are private sector individuals (firms) involved in the operation of the program?

7. To what extent, if any, is there union involvement with the project? At a minimum, such projects are to have approval of the relevant labor organization in the area before they are funded. However, the range we have heard of is from joint union-company projects to organized objection to projects by unions.

8. Program Services – Please describe the services being provided by this project (e.g., OJT, classroom training, job search) and the relative emphasis being placed on the various services. Is there a single service sequence for the participants or are multiple and/or sequential services provided? [A good way to characterize the service mix would be the number of participants in each type of service at a point in time.] Are there particular entry requirements (e.g., H.S. diploma, recent work experience) for particular program activities?

9. Please describe the kinds of services provided in the various program activities. For example, if the activity is OJT, the kinds of occupations and firms in which the participants are placed; if it is classroom training, the kinds of educational or skill classes that are offered. What is the length of the various program services? Do they vary for different participants? Are these services different (in length, content, skill level) from those offered under Title IIA?

10. To what extent is counseling an important component of this project? Three types of counseling are most important for this purpose. The first is job search skills training for participants who have substantial work experience but have not been in the job market in recent years. The second is counseling experienced workers who may have been in high paying manufacturing jobs concerning the wage levels they may expect to receive. The third is personal counseling for dealing with unemployment and related problems.

Part IV. Program Participants

This section is composed of two parts. The first is a narrative description of the participants in the program and the way in which they are selected for participation. The second is the table on the next page that asks you to indicate, to the extent that the data are available, the numerical characteristics of the participants. We are primarily interested in demographics, education and prior work experience. If possible, this should correspond to the TY84. However, if this is a new project, first quarter PY84 data may be available.

1. Please characterize the participants in the program. Where do they come from, what kinds of jobs have they held, etc.? Are all eligible participants enrolled in the program or are certain groups given priority or selected for particular program services? If particular individuals are "selected in or out," on what basis is this done? What is "different" about these workers relative to those eligible for Title IIA?

Part V. Program Outcomes

1. What kind of job development/placement process is used to place participants in jobs postprogram? The range of possibilities here may include everything from individual job search by the participants to job development done by program staff to prior agreements with particular employers to hire program participants. Does the placement process differ by program activity or subcontractor? How effective do these processes appear to be? What kinds of firms/organizations are targeted for placement of program participants? Where does relocation fit in as a placement strategy?

2. To the extent that it is available, we would like to include the following outcome information. If available, please break it down by program activity. Does this project have any State/SDA imposed performance standards that it is to meet or performance levels built into its contract? What kinds of jobs account for the placement?

Average wage at entry
   (of those placed at termination)_____
Average wage at termination (of those placed)_____
Cost per placement_____
Proportion of terminees placed_____

Table 1. Enrollment and Participant Characteristics
Period: _____ to _____

Total Participants

Total Terminations
  Entered employment
  other positive terminations
  other terminations

Characteristics

Sex
  Male
  Female

Age
  14–15
  16–19
  20–21
  22–44
  45–54
  55 and over

Education
  School dropout
  Student (H.S. or less)
  High school graduate or more

Race
  White
  Black
  Hispanic
  Native American
  Asian

Employment Barriers
  Limited English
  Handicapped
  Offender
  Other

Benefit Recipiency
  U.I. Claimant
  U.I. Exhaustee
  Public Assistance (GA)
  AFDC
  Youth AFDC

Labor Force Status (prior 26 weeks)
  Unemployed 1–14 weeks
  Unemployed 15 or more weeks
  Not in labor force

Part VI: Overall Assessment

1. Are there particular aspects of this project that are important to its operation effectiveness, outcome statistics, etc.? Are there particular aspects that might be important to development of programs for dislocated workers? Are there particular problems that adversely affected implementation, effectiveness or outcomes that you consider an important part of the assessment of the project and which we have not adequately covered elsewhere in this report form?

2. Please provide your overall assessment of the project, its appropriateness to the eligible client population being served and to the industries from which participants are selected and into which attempts are made to place them or to the labor market in which the program operates. Succinctly put, is the program, in your view, appropriate to the problem? Why or why not?

DATE DUE